GW00691435

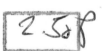

WITHDRAWN FROM STOCK
OFFERED FOR SALE
WITH ANY FAULTS BY
CITY OF WESTMINSTER LIBRARIES

PRICE 2.50p

WITHDRAWN FROM STOCK

CITY OF WESTMINSTER LIBRARIES

PRICE

NORMA

NORMA

A Biography

Tim Walker

FOURTH ESTATE · *London*

CGD-L

BRO 5|93

First published in Great Britain in 1993 by
Fourth Estate Limited
289 Westbourne Grove
London W11 2QA

Copyright © 1993 by Tim Walker

The right of Tim Walker to be identified as the author of
this work has been asserted by him in accordance with the
Copyright, Designs and Patents Act 1988.

A catalogue record for this book is available from the
British Library.

ISBN 1–85702–063–4

All rights reserved. No part of this publication may be
reproduced, transmitted, or stored in a retrieval system, in
any form or by any means, without permission in writing from
Fourth Estate Limited.

Typeset by York House Typographic Ltd, London W13
Printed in Great Britain by   Hartnolls Ltd, Bodmin

For my mother and father

Contents

Photographs

NORMA

Acknowledgements

I AM INDEBTED to Eileen MacDonald for giving me the confidence to write this book.

For their counsel, encouragement and support, I should like to thank Jane Carr, my editor at Fourth Estate, and my agent Julian Alexander of Jacintha Alexander Associates. I should also like to express my admiration for Vicky Barnsley for having the courage to take a risk not merely on a new author, but also on a figure whose continued presence in the public eye was subject to the vicissitudes of political life.

It might seem strange, considering the war of words in which we have latterly become embroiled, but I consider it appropriate too to thank Mrs Major. It was my intention to write this as an authorised biography, but, when that turned out not to be possible, Mrs Major was kind enough not to raise any objections when I approached her innumerable friends and colleagues for interviews, thereby making my job easier than it might otherwise have been.

Charles Garside, my editor at the *European*, deserves a special mention for permitting me to go off and write it (and, more pertinently, having me back when I finished), as does Herbert Pearson, the paper's managing editor, for his steadfast support. I am grateful too to the political journalist Nigel Dudley for inducting me, with great patience and skill, into the ways of modern parliamentarians and their servants.

For their valuable insights, I should especially like to thank: Bruce Anderson, Jane Ashdown, Robert and Dulcie Atkins, Olive Baddeley, Jim and Betty Bartlett, Baroness Blatch, June Bronhill, Peter Brown, Stella Brown, Lady Bruce-Gardyne, Lady Callaghan, Ian Cameron Black, Alastair Campbell, Bette Caunt, Arthur Chandler, Michael Crick, Patricia Crittenden, John Cunningham, Barbara Daly, Nick Davies, Lord Deedes, Ian Denson, Pat Dessoy, Elizabeth Dix, Chris Donat, Richard Finny, June Fisher, Peter Golds, The Duchess of Grafton, Joe Green, William Hague, Edith Hall, Pauline Hallanzy, Gladys Harper, Edna Healey, Fred Heddell, Sheila Herbert, David Hill, Alicia Hollings, Joyce Hopkirk, Judy Hurd, Margaret Jay, Clive Jones, Rosemary Juggins, Barbara Kent of the Wagstaff Society, Glenys Kinnock, The Rev. Ronald Lancaster, Roger Law, Rhona Livingstone, Jean Lucas, Sir Ian McKellen, Terry Major-Ball, Margaret Marshall, Beryl Matthews, Stella Matthews, David and Judy Mellor, Chris Moncrieff, Sheila Murphy, Joy and Geoff Murray, Pre Newbon, Derek Oakley, Bernard Perkins, Lord Renton, Lord Rix, David Rogers, Dr Dorothy Rowe, Patricia Salt, Maggie Scott, Catherine Shadbolt, Gladys Simpson, Anne Smart, Victor Smart, John Steel, Carole Stone, Heather Strudwick, Dame Joan Sutherland, John Sweeney, Harvey Thomas, Andrew Thomson, Carina Trimingham, Derek Wall, Barbara Wallis, Sally Weale, Rosalind Whateley, Pat Wheeler, Des Wilson, Sue Winn and many others, who, for their own reasons, wish to remain anonymous.

I am particularly grateful to my fellow author Nesta Wyn Ellis for generously allowing me access to hitherto unpublished transcripts of her own extensive series of interviews with Mrs Major.

To Bob Turner, Kate Hodges, Lorraine Took, Jeffrey Care and Nick Robinson, who helped me in my research, and Delia

ACKNOWLEDGEMENTS

Culpan, who provided secretarial assistance, I should also like to record my gratitude.

Since my principal qualification for being commissioned to write this book was my career in newspapers, I should finally like to acknowledge the great debt that I owe to the following people for keeping it on the rails for the past ten years — John Bryant, Ray Horsfield, Anthony Howard, Ian Mather, Terry Page, Ian Watson and David Williams.

Tim Walker, London, 1993

Prologue

FRIDAY, 6 SEPTEMBER 1991: The Prime Minister's gleaming black Daimler draws up outside Ridgeon's, a firm of builders' merchants in Tenison Road, Cambridge, and John Major and his wife Norma, accompanied by a small army of personal detectives, walk purposefully into the building.

The staff at Ridgeon's and the other shoppers watch in bemused silence as the Majors set about a painstaking inspection of the bidets, jacuzzis and porcelain toilets on display. To everyone present, it is clear that Norma is in the mood for some serious shopping.

A local newspaper reporter, who arrives on the scene with impressive speed, walks up to the Prime Minister and asks him what he is doing. 'We are here looking at bathrooms for our home,' Mr Major tells him, 'but we haven't made a final decision on which range we are choosing yet. We are just considering a few ideas.'

Making the most of the opportunity, the reporter then asks him if he would care to end the speculation surrounding the date of the General Election. 'No, I'm not going to give a date for the General Election yet,' Mr Major replies, obviously becoming a little irritated by the man's presence. 'I'd much rather stick to talking about bathrooms.'

The detectives insert themselves deftly between Mr Major and the reporter and the man duly withdraws. Before he leaves, he elicits a few comments from some of the other shoppers for his story. One old woman tells him: 'I went in to look at kitchen sinks and was astonished to see Mrs Major in deep conversation with a man in a grey suit, whom I took to be a salesman. They were looking at a very expensive jacuzzi. I couldn't believe it when the "salesman" turned round – and it was the Prime Minister.'

It was Norma's idea to go shopping at Ridgeon's. She had been going on at John for some time about the bathroom, and, for once having him there in the car with her as they drove home to Huntingdon, she thought the chance was too good to miss.

What was remarkable about the visit was that it came just hours after the two of them had touched down at Heathrow at the end of a diplomatic mission which had seen John move from holiday talks with President Bush at the summer White House, through a Moscow in ferment, to facing down the Chinese leaders on human rights in Peking.

That was all very well, but for Norma the state of her bathroom was a matter which the Prime Minister couldn't put off a moment longer. For her, that was 'real life', after all.

CHAPTER 1

The Dresden Doll

S UCH A LUCKY little girl, Mrs Edith Hall used to think when she peered down at Norma in her pram. She had a beautiful, caring mother, a handsome, hard-working father, and one of the loveliest villages in the country in which to grow up.

Of an afternoon, Mrs Hall would often stop and have a chat with Mrs Wagstaff as she wheeled her bonny little baby around All Stretton. They would talk about this and that: the new films that were showing at the Regal, the dance nights at the village hall, but most of all they would talk about Norma, because Mrs Wagstaff was uncommonly proud of her baby. 'I must admit that she was a very angelic little thing,' says Mrs Hall, now ninety and still living in the area. 'She always used to smile at me whenever I came up, but then I got the impression that she seemed to be smiling almost all the time. I don't think that I ever heard her cry once.'

The tranquil Shropshire village had a curiously timeless quality about it in 1942, the year of Norma's birth. It was a place of oak-beamed cottages, whitewashed walls, and neighbours who knew everybody's business and had the time to talk about it. The pace of life was dictated by the seasons, and the surrounding patchwork of fields afforded the village not only its income, but also its character.

Henry Adams used to speak about the curious 'absence of evolution' in Shropshire, and certainly nothing ever seemed to change in All Stretton. The nearest any of Adolf Hitler's bombs came was when the Squirrel Inn at Bridgnorth took a direct hit one Saturday lunchtime and several of the regulars were killed. Other than that, there was little to remind the villagers that the country was at war.

Norma Christina Elizabeth Wagstaff was born on 12 February at the Lady Forester Hospital in the nearby town of Much Wenlock. Edith Wagstaff had come to All Stretton with her husband Norman, a sergeant in the Royal Artillery, after he had been posted to the area as part of the war effort. The Wagstaffs had married at Bermondsey Register Office on 18 November 1939, just two months after Prime Minister Neville Chamberlain had announced that Britain was at war with Germany. Norman had been twenty-three, Edith nineteen.

Edith's early life in London was a world away from All Stretton and its genteel lifestyle. Her late father Roland Johnson, a dock labourer, had died of a heart attack when she was just eight years old, and her mother, Victoria, had had to raise her single-handedly in her tiny flat in Bermondsey on a piteously low wage from a munitions factory. Just before she married Norman, Edith had herself been bringing some money into the home as an umbrella saleswoman.

Norman, the son of Reuel Wagstaff, a retired police constable with the Metropolitan Police, and Elizabeth, a tailoress, was a tall, attractive man with thick brilliantined hair and a fashionable Ronald Colman moustache. In civilian life he had been a machine manager at a firm of letterpress printers, but he was doing his bit for his country as an auxiliary fireman by the time he married Edith.

In an uncertain time, the couple had had the courage to look to the future. When the war was over, Norman told his bride, he would realise his ambition to become a professional pianist. And it was Edith's ambition to raise a family.

Norman was lucky with his first posting. His days living in All Stretton with Edith and his baby daughter were the happiest of his life. The family could not have wanted for a better landlady than the local postmistress, Hilda Evans, a plump, warm-hearted lady who lived above the shop with her husband Cyril and their three boisterous children, Catherine, Ron and Brian. Mrs Evans made the Wagstaffs treat the house as if it was their own, and it wasn't long before she became a firm friend. The friendship was sealed when Edith asked her to be Norma's godmother, an honour that she was delighted to accept. 'It was a very happy little household,' Mrs Evans's daughter Catherine Shadbolt says. 'For all of us, it was a marvellous, care-free time, and, in many ways, we became one big family. We all ate together and played together. During the long, hot summers, I was often out in the garden with Aunty Edie and Norma.'

The Wagstaffs settled in well. Joe Green, in those days the teenaged son of the owners of the general store, recalls that Norman and Edith were a well-liked couple in the village. 'They made a real effort to become a part of the community, and, unlike a lot of the brasher, less respectful servicemen who ended up here, they were quickly accepted by the locals,' he says. 'My father often had a pint with Sergeant Wagstaff at the Yew Tree pub. Everybody liked him – he was always the sort of fellow to be first to get a round in. Once he made a giant scale model of a sailing ship which he let me play with in his garden.'

Derek Wall, another local teenager at the time, often saw the Wagstaffs on nights out at the Regal Cinema over at Stretton. 'Norman and Edith had a lot of fun here,' says Mr Wall. 'Quite a few of the servicemen who had come up from London took a while to adjust to the life here, but then of course most of them didn't have their families with them as Norman had.' On Satur-day nights, he remembers, the Wagstaffs went to the large village hall which the Royal Artillery had built in the meadow, dancing – 'rather impressively,' he says – to the tunes of 'In the Mood' and 'Moonlight Serenade': 'I suppose you could say that they were quite a glamorous couple, at least by the standards of the village.'

The family's idyll was unexpectedly shattered towards the end of the war, when Norman, a second lieutenant by this stage and commanding his own battery, received a new posting. The papers, always kept vague for reasons of national security, said that he was destined for 'Western Europe'. Along with everybody else in the village, Edith knew very well that her husband was being thrown into one of the bloodiest of the remaining battlefields, but she bore the news with great fortitude. 'She wasn't the type of woman who would complain about anything,' says Mr Wall. 'If she had her fears, then she kept them to herself.'

After Norman had gone, Edith decided that it was no time to take Norma back to the family home in Bermondsey and instead took her to live with her husband's aunt, Mrs Louise Hall, at her cottage in Bourn. The village, not far from Cambridge, was every bit as beautiful as All Stretton, but not of course so well insulated from the realities of the war. On many nights, Edith and Norma could hear the bombs falling. They prayed for Norman each night.

In Bourn, on New Year's Day 1944, Edith gave birth to a son, Colin Desmond Wagstaff. Just six days later, he died of bronchopneumonia, then a common cause of death in infancy. Mrs Beryl Matthews, a friend and neighbour in the village who had herself lost a baby in similar circumstances, said that it was not something which Edith ever felt able to talk about. Her other neighbours never knew about the tragedy.

The following year Victory in Europe was declared on 7 May and Edith thanked God that her husband had made it through the war and would shortly be coming home for good. Just six days later, by a cruel stroke of irony, she received a telegram informing her that he had been killed in a motorcycle accident. He had just celebrated his twenty-ninth birthday.

His death, coming so soon after her son's, left Mrs Wagstaff desolate. She returned to London with Norma to live in her late husband's small flat in Abbey Buildings, a forbidding Victorian block in Abbey Street, Bermondsey. The block had a reputation for the bad types who lived there and the accommodation was basic: there was no heating, the lavatory was on the landing and the walls were paper thin which meant that it was difficult to sleep. Mrs Wagstaff's financial circumstances were not as desperate as most of her neighbours' however. The proceeds from her husband's personal effects had amounted to £504.2s, a not inconsiderable sum in 1945, and, on top of that, there was her war widow's pension of £3 per week.

Even so, Mrs Wagstaff decided within months of her husband's death to take not one but three part-time jobs as a book-keeper, finding in her work a way of coping with her bereavement. To enable her to put in such long hours, she packed her four-year-old daughter off to a now defunct boarding-school in Bexhill-on-Sea, which she was able to pay for with the help of Royal Artillery charities. After Norma had gone, she took in a lodger, one Beryl Laine. Norma was not permitted to come home even during the school holidays, but would be placed with elderly relatives so that her mother could continue with her work. That she shut Norma so comprehensively out of her life suggests that she may initially have found her too painful a reminder of her late husband.

Norma was not old enough to feel resentful, but the lack of any real home life did, however, appear to have a profound psychological effect on her. A lot of her time was spent playing with her dolls' house, poignantly creating in her imagination the family life that she had herself been denied: Mummy, Daddy and their daughter, all together under one roof, as it should be. She had a lot of dolls. She remembers one in particular: 'I treated it like a baby. It was fed from a bottle at the right time and its nappies were washed out and hung on the line.' Her childhood dreams reflected a deep-rooted sense of insecurity. In one she was walking precariously along a pier, with large gaps between the slats so that she could see the turbulent, inky black water far, far below. Another had her at the top of a long slide, again on a pier, just about to shoot helplessly down to some distant watery abyss. The worst of all – a recurring one – had her waking up and finding a snake in her bed. In none of the dreams, of course, was there anyone for her to turn to for help. She was all alone in a sinister and perilous world. Little Norma began to fear the dark so intensely that the school matron permitted her to leave her dormitory to sleep in a fully-lit room.

At the age of seven, Norma was uprooted again and sent to Oakfield School, a private co-educational establishment in Dulwich, where she was one of only eight girls who boarded. Mrs Rhona Livingstone, the headmaster's wife, recalls that she was 'a nice, friendly little girl with lovely eyes. Academically, a bit of a disappointment, but no dimwit'. Not all the teachers were quite so enamoured of her. One, a Miss Bensell, used to shout at her, and at times succeeded in turning her to jelly. Only one thing frightened her more than Miss Bensell – and that was being left on her own. Her worst moment at the school was when she inadvertently detached herself from the end of a crocodile of girls out walking in streets some miles from the school. Her teacher went back and found her sitting alone on a wall, bawling her eyes out. The nights in the dormitory were ordeals for her too. All the other girls seemed to be bigger than her, and she says they used to terrify her by 'bouncing about' in the dark.

Arthur Chandler, her history teacher, says that she had reminded him of a Dresden doll: 'a pretty little thing with her two pony tails, but, I always felt, terribly delicate.' He considered her 'good to outstanding at English'. She appears to have made little impression upon her classmates. 'One just remembered that she was there, but nothing else about her remains in my mind,' says a contemporary, Patricia Salt. So too the school's most famous old boy, Michael Crawford, who says that he had no idea she had been at the school at the same time as him. Norma, by her own admission, was a rather bossy little girl, more concerned with ensuring that everything was neat and tidy than with making friends. During the holidays, she never brought any of her classmates home, no doubt self-conscious about the fact that most of them had bigger and more expensive homes than hers. She used to hate it when the Sunday night came when she had to return to school.

Norma's 11-plus exam at Oakfield was not encouraging, and her mother, no longer receiving financial assistance from the Royal Artillery, reluctantly had to transfer her to a state school, Peckham School for Girls, where her name appeared on the register as Norma Johnson. Her mother had chosen to revert to her maiden name after becoming estranged from her in-laws. Her relationship with Reuel and Elizabeth Wagstaff, who also had a flat in Abbey Buildings, had not been easy since Norman's death and latterly they had argued over whether it had been right to send Norma to boarding-school at such a tender age. So bitter had the exchanges been that Edith felt she could no longer bear to call herself a Wagstaff.

It wasn't just a new surname that Norma had to adjust to at Peckham. The imposing red-brick school, built in the grounds of an old asylum, must have seemed a hostile, horribly alien environment after the two rather cosy private establishments which she had previously attended. There were 1,500 girls on the roll, a lot of them from poor, broken homes in one of London's toughest catchment areas. The way Norma had been taught to speak and carry herself at her old schools made her suddenly look desperately out of place. (It says a lot that the school's second most famous old girl, after Norma, is Lorraine Chase, the streetwise Cockney 'wafted' to paradise from Luton Airport in the Campari adverts.)

As a day girl, however, Norma did have the consolation of having her own home to return to in the evenings. Mrs Johnson, who had moved to a modest two-bedroomed flat in Anerley Park in Penge, was invariably out working when Norma returned, but Norma would busy herself with the housework. 'There was nothing I liked better than cleaning out a cupboard,' she recalls. Mrs Johnson kept a close eye on Norma's progress at the school and made sure that she didn't get in with the wrong crowd. Her daughter swiftly became a favourite of the doughty head-mistress, Anne Smart, who felt from their first meeting that she had potential, despite the fact that her 11-plus result card from Oakfield had been marked at the bottom 'not suitable for academic study'. With Miss Smart's encouragement, Norma was soon able to prove them wrong. June Fisher, her history teacher, says that she was 'a good, quiet student, who tackled her studies with a sense of urgency. She always seemed to have her nose buried in a book.'

Like so many children who switch from boarding- to day-school, Norma found the adjustment difficult; all of a sudden, she didn't have every hour of her life planned for her. A neighbour at Anerley Park, Mrs Gladys Harper, remembers that she didn't go out much in the evenings like the other girls in the area. According to Mrs Harper, Norma was a real home-body who spent almost every evening in with her mother, sewing, reading, doing her homework, or – a particular joy – listening to *Friday Night is Music Night* on the radio. On the rare occasions that she did go out, it was with her mother, usually to the local Conservative Club, principally because it was handy and the drinks were cheap. Norma and her mother would never drink anything alcoholic – Mrs Harper chuckles at the very suggestion. 'They just sat quietly and chatted,' she says. On Norma's birth-day, as a special treat, she would go with her mother to Lyon's Corner House for tea.

At the school Pauline Glover, a fellow student, saw Norma as aloof and lonely, but seeking no one's company. 'I don't remember Norma ever having been a part of a pair, or a merry, laughing group,' she says. 'I can't really remember her being particularly friends with anyone. If you spoke with a middle-class accent in Peckham, you ran the gauntlet a bit. It made you defensive. But Norma did seem to have an instinct to get in with people whom it would be advantageous for her to get in with. She certainly seemed to be very close to the headmistress.'

Norma's popularity probably wasn't boosted by her elevation to the role of head girl at the age of eighteen. When she was offered the post by Miss Smart, she accepted without hesitation. 'She had no doubts about whether she could do it,' Miss Smart recalls. 'She was a young lady with a good opinion of herself.' Traditionally head girls at Peckham were elected by their fellow prefects but, in Norma's case, Pauline got the impression that the headmistress had personally intervened during the selection process. Norma had succeeded a girl called Elaine Kelly who was popular with the students and in tune with what they were thinking. The trouble was that the staff considered her to be a shade too much in tune, and so, when she left, it was felt that a less familiar figure was required. Correct, well-spoken Norma seemed to fit the bill exactly: in Miss Smart's words, 'an excellent ambassadress for the school'.

At the school's speech day in the autumn, Norma was called upon to deliver a speech. She acquitted herself well, despite the size of her audience, and even managed an apposite quote, albeit a rather obscure one, believed to have originated with a turn-of-the-century writer by the name of J. Mason Knox:

> It ain't the guns or armaments
> Or the money they can pay,
> It's the close co-operation
> That makes them win the day.
> It ain't the individual,
> Nor the army as a whole,
> But the everlastin' teamwork
> Of every bloomin' soul.

11

The words went straight over the heads of most of her fellow students, but to Norma, at that moment, they clearly had a particular resonance. It was to all intents and purposes an appeal for help – if she was going to be head girl, then everybody was going to have to muck in. Miss Smart feels that the speech was a huge success. 'It was,' she says, 'a very good, very dignified performance. It was well-written and well-delivered, and set precisely the right tone.' Pauline Glover was not, however, entirely certain whether the Cockney accent with which Norma invested her quotation was an unconditional success. This was the only occasion that Pauline could remember when Norma actually did anything as head girl. 'Apart from that speech, I can't remember her doing very much at all,' she recalls. 'She had a policy of getting involved as little as possible and was definitely not a girl who wanted to change the world. She knew where she was going in life, and to her, at that point, everything appeared to be going according to plan, and there was no point in rocking the boat.'

When Pauline succeeded Norma as head girl at Peckham she did not consider her a hard act to follow. 'I do not think that she was terribly effective as head girl. She was not tough, and I think at that school at that time, you needed to be tough.' Miss Smart agrees that Norma was not as impressive in the role as her successor: 'Norma could not think on her feet in the way that Pauline could, but I had no regrets about appointing her. She brought calm and dignity to the school at a time when it was going through tremendous change. To that extent, she did the school a great service.'

Norma, for her part, says that she left the school with 'grateful memories'. Her ambition had at first been to become a nanny – she had been accepted by the prestigious Norland College – but, latterly, she had decided, like most of her fellow sixth-formers, to become a teacher. The seven O-levels and two A-levels (geography and needlework) that she passed at Peckham won her a place on a teacher-training course at Battersea College of Domestic Science at Clapham Common Northside. She was particularly strong in dressmaking, a skill in her family since her grandmother, Elizabeth Wagstaff, had been a tailoress. The old woman had passed on some of her talents to Norma during her years in Bermondsey. As Norma recalls, Elizabeth used to sit cross-legged on the darning table sewing flies in men's trousers. She had Norma making her own clothes by the time she was twelve.

Norma worked hard during her three years at the college. Beryl Matthews, her old friend from her days in Bourn, remembers her coming back to stay with her some weekends when she needed a break. Almost all she did when she got there was sleep. When she finally got up she would read books — textbooks mostly, but occasionally some escapist, romantic fiction, such as stories about the Knights of the Round Table. She would also play with Mrs Matthews's six-month-old daughter Stella. Norma loved children. She used to say that from the first day she could speak, she wanted to be a nanny. Mrs Matthews says that unfortunately almost every time she picked Stella up she made her cry.

Whatever time Norma had to herself in London was invariably spent at the theatre. She had graduated from pantomime, which she had adored as a toddler, to serious theatre when she went on a school visit to the Old Vic to see Judi Dench and John Neville in a production of *Hamlet*. During her years at college she attended all the new shows, often going to the first nights, always in the cheapest seats.

It was, however, when she visited the opera that she decided she had been initiated into a higher art form. The bravura productions and the larger-than-life stars in their heavy make-up and flamboyant costumes exerted an immediate and powerful hold over her. The opera was a social as much as a cultural pastime and it brought her a motley collection of new friends — among them Peter Golds, a teenager whom she had first set eyes on in rather inauspicious circumstances during a performance of

The Daughter of the Regiment at Covent Garden. As Golds recalls, Norma and her mother were sitting in the row behind him and a group of his friends, and were staring daggers because they had committed the cardinal sin of talking after the curtain had gone up.

To say that Norma became obsessive about opera would not be an over-statement. She would go about three times a week, turning up outside the opera houses with her Thermos and sleeping bag and cheerfully bedding down for the night to be first in line for the best value tickets the following day. Often it was enough just to arrive at the crack of dawn, but when a major star like Joan Sutherland was performing, there was no alternative but to join the queue the night before. Her mother never worried when she didn't come home: she always knew where she would be.

A remarkably good sleeper, Norma managed to doze even as the lorries were trundling past and the early morning shift workers picked their way over her and her possessions. Golds, who would often share street space with her, says that even in such undignified circumstances, she never lost her sense of decorum. 'When she woke up, she would stroll into one of the grand hotels nearby – the Strand Palace was a particular favourite – to use their toilets and powder rooms,' he recalls. 'I think a lot of other people would have liked to have done that too, but they realised that they couldn't have carried it off in the way she could. She seemed to be to the manor born and of course nobody ever dreamt of asking her whether she was a guest.'

London's regular opera-goers thought of themselves very much as a family. They would sleep together (on the pavements, outside the opera houses, as a rule), eat and drink together, and, because tickets to any one production were often limited to four per person, they would buy tickets for each other and surreptitiously trade them outside so that they could attend all the performances they wanted. If Sutherland was giving seven performances, a real Sutherland fan would of course want to be in attendance at *all* seven. Within the 'family' there were inevitably squabbles, occasionally over seats, but mostly factional differences between the fans of Callas and the fans of Sutherland, her arch-rival. It was not possible among these people to be a fan of Sutherland *and* Callas any more than it was possible to have two religions. The passions aroused were such that zealots in the Sutherland camp would not be above going to a performance given by Callas with the sole intention of booing or coughing at the worst possible moments. Callas fans would then retaliate by doing the same to Sutherland.

Norma was very much a Sutherland fan. She was first on her feet at the end of her performances, frantically throwing daffodils down on to the stage. Then she would run round to the back to secure the best place at the stage door to be ready for the magical moment when the star emerged to greet 'the kids', as she used to call her devotees. Sutherland saw Norma out there on so many nights, just watching or asking her to sign one of her record sleeves, that it wasn't long before she was actually greeting her by her first name, a considerable honour. 'And how are you, Norma?' she would say. 'I hope you are looking after yourself, darling.' She used to worry, rather endearingly, that Norma wasn't feeding herself properly. She didn't see how she could be – she *always* seemed to be at Covent Garden.

For Norma, it was a happy, carefree time. When she bought herself a second-hand white Mini, she soon had the idea of using it to transport her and her friends to some of the great opera houses of Europe. She went to The Hague to see Sutherland, and, in a plan devised at the very last minute, to Hamburg to see an opulent production of *Giulio Cesare*. Norma packed into her car Alicia Gains, a lanky student whom she had met while queuing for tickets to see Sutherland at the Royal Festival Hall, and two giggly Australian girls called Joy and Edna, and the four of them set off one dark, rainy Friday night with a sign attached to the boot saying 'Hamburg or bust'. It was an eventful journey. They had to get to Harwich to catch the ferry, but somehow managed to get on to the road to Clacton. 'We're not going to make it in time,' Norma kept saying, as she tried desperately to find her way back on to the road to Harwich, the town's lights maddeningly visible in the distance; so near and yet so far. Alicia kept reassuring her that she had nothing to worry about. 'We'll make it,' Alicia said, a declaration of blind faith if ever there was one. 'No, we won't,' Norma replied glumly. Joy and Edna just giggled.

They finally reached Harwich, broke a few speed limits as they raced through the town, and got on to the ramp of the ferry with just seconds to spare before it was raised. On the other side of the Channel, they got lost again on the autoroute, having taken the wrong slip road before Hamburg, and might have continued on their way had not four young men in a car come alongside them and shouted that if it was true what the sign at the back of their car said, then they had better do a U-turn quickly. When they finally arrived in Hamburg, rather the worse for wear, Norma's face fell when it turned out that Joy and Edna had come with hardly any money at all, which meant that they all ended up staying in a rather seedy pension. But the performance that evening made it all seem worthwhile. The next day, on the Sunday, before beginning the return journey, Norma was adamant that she was going to have one proper meal while she was in Hamburg. She and Alicia quietly gave Joy and Edna the slip and went out to dine in the grand manner at one of the big hotels.

Norma continued to go to the opera three nights a week after she secured her first job at St Michael and All Angels Church of England School in Camberwell where she taught domestic science and needlework. Even though she often found herself doing a full day's work after spending a night on the pavement outside Covent Garden, she acquired a reputation as a conscientious and diligent teacher. Her colleagues got the impression, however, that she was not especially happy in her work. Her real problem was that she could not keep order, one recalls. 'It got around among the pupils that you could misbehave in her classes, and, of course, that was fatal.' Alicia says she felt that Norma had gone into teaching with the best of intentions but found the reality of an inner-London school frustrating and soul-destroying. 'She soon found that some of the kids just didn't want to learn,' she says. 'And even if she put 120 per cent of effort into it, she was still going to get two fingers pointed up at her.' Norma herself remarked that she found her students 'Bolshie'.

Norma's salary at the school meant that she soon had enough money to buy herself a one-bedroomed flat in a block just around the corner from where her mother lived in Anerley Park. On her very first night she invoked the ire of her neighbours who banged on her walls in the early hours as she and Alicia tried their hand at some urgently-needed DIY work. Norma soon settled in, however, decorating the flat, so Alicia says, with some flair, even on a tight budget. Alicia and Peter Golds were both regulars at the flat, though Norma seldom cooked for them, preferring instead to sit around with them drinking cups of coffee, and talking, inevitably, about opera. Sometimes Norma would make costume dolls, a little hobby of hers.

Peter and Alicia were both Conservative activists and some-times they succeeded in persuading Norma to muck in during the local election campaigns. Politics didn't excite her in the way it excited Peter and Alicia – to them, tickets to a count were to be cherished as much as tickets to see Sutherland – but she usually tagged along to keep them quiet. Alicia was certain that Norma supported the cause, but added that she was not so rabidly Conservative that she couldn't socialise with Liberals and Socialists, but then, she points out, in the parts of London that she was moving in, she would not have had many people to talk to if she had taken that attitude.

There was not much else that Norma and her friends did besides going to the opera, drinking coffee and watching TV or putting in the odd stint for the local Tories – simple, wholesome activities by the standards of the time. As Alicia puts it: 'This was the sixties and the "Permissive Society" seemed to be raging around us. We just thought: "Well, if they want to behave like that, they can. It's nothing to do with us."' They knew very well, she adds, that some of the people they were mixing with were getting up to all sorts of things, with all sorts of people, but none of them ever let a disapproving word past their lips. 'You can't tell people how to live their lives,' says Alicia. 'We'd have sounded like terrible prigs if we had.'

In addition to Sutherland, Norma had a penchant for the beautiful June Bronhill, who was at the time considered a comparable star. In 1964, Norma was a regular at the Lyric Theatre where Miss Bronhill was appearing alongside Keith Michell and Donald Wolfit in *Robert and Elizabeth*, a hugely successful musical version of *The Barretts of Wimpole Street*. Miss Bronhill remembers Norma asking for her autograph one night and then spotted her outside the stage door several nights running.

Seeing Norma looking thoroughly bedraggled in heavy rain as she left the theatre on one occasion, Miss Bronhill took pity on her and said that the next time she came she could come into her dressing room for a chat after the performance. Norma was in the following night, and, surprisingly, the gregarious Australian star, noted for her colourful vocabulary, warmed to her shy, diffident fan. As Miss Bronhill puts it: 'A lot of my fans tended to be all over me like a mad woman's knitting – but not Norma. She wasn't in the least bit gushy and that made a change. I'm a Cancerian and I guess it must have been the home-lover in her that appealed to me.'

After that first meeting, Miss Bronhill instructed the man on the stage door to let Norma come in to see her whenever she wished. Norma had made it on to June's List: a select group of dedicated fans to whom Miss Bronhill granted private audiences after her shows. 'We were all thrilled to get on it,' said Mrs Pat Perkins, who was also on the list. 'We'd have a few minutes with her to talk about the show, but sometimes she would simply be too tired and when we came along she would say: "I'm sorry darlings, but I'm absolutely buggered tonight", and we'd have to let her be.' Norma came in often and developed something of a crush on the show's star. Once she surprised Miss Bronhill by presenting her with a gigantic strawberry dessert which she called 'Bronhill's Fool'. 'It was quite delicious, and, like a fool, I ate almost all of it,' Miss Bronhill jokes. And then, when Miss Bronhill casually remarked how worn-out her stage gown was beginning to look, Norma went off without saying a word and made her a brand new one. The costume department weren't entirely happy about an outsider making such an elaborate period dress, but when Miss Bronhill put it on, they could not fault it. 'Her kindnesses took me aback,' Miss Bronhill says. 'She was one of the nicest, sweetest women I had ever come across.'

June Bronhill was married to Richard Finny, an engaging, plain-speaking Australian who was working as a director for BBC TV News. Their respective jobs meant that they were seldom at home and they therefore had to engage a series of live-in nannies to look after their baby daughter Carolyn who was, by all accounts, a little terror. When their latest nanny resigned, Miss Bronhill suggested offering the job to Norma. The idea did not go down well with her husband. Finny took the view that there would be no more peace for either of them if any of June's Groupies – as he used disparagingly to call his wife's fans – were allowed into the house, or even given their home telephone number. As he recalls: 'They could be a bit over-powering at times. I guess I could never really make them out. I often *had* to see June in the same show over and over again, but these characters did it voluntarily.'

Finny had met Norma, whom he had found painfully shy and lacking in self-confidence: 'I guess in those days she was living her life through June in a way. I rather suspected that somewhere inside her she wanted to be a big opera star herself. It struck me as a bit sad really.' With little time to find anyone else, Finny finally relented and Norma was offered the position. Even though she knew that it would mean giving up her job at the school where she had worked for five years, she accepted without hesitation.

Norma moved into the couple's mews cottage in Harriet Walk, Knightsbridge, and if Finny still had any doubts she soon dispelled them. 'I have to say that in many ways Norma was a better mother to Carolyn during the time she worked for us than my wife was,' he says. 'June was inclined to spoil her, whereas Norma took her in hand and saw to it she didn't get out of control. She was also a fairly good cook.'

Life at Harriet Walk must have been a revelation for Norma. Miss Bronhill and her husband had frequent parties attended by colourful theatrical folk, and, on the rare occasions when they weren't entertaining, they would often engage in loud, stagey rows, more out of habit than any genuine animosity. According to Miss Bronhill, nothing that Norma heard or saw ever fazed her. 'I don't remember Norma ever swearing herself, but she was certainly no prude,' she recalls. 'In fact I often caught her trying to suppress a giggle after I'd told a rather risqué joke. She was fun to have around.'

CHAPTER 2

A Fine Romance

JUNE BRONHILL still remembers the night in 1970 when Norma burst into her dressing room flushed with excitement and announced: 'I've just met the most wonderful man — and I think I am in love.'

By this stage, Miss Bronhill knew Norma well enough to feel protective towards her. There had been a man in Norma's life before, a somewhat flamboyant character who had worn braces, a hand-knitted V-necked tank top and carried a purse, but he had, Norma admits, broken her heart. June naturally tried to find out as much as she could about this new paragon whom Norma was speaking about so excitedly. She was able to establish that he worked for a bank, did something quite important on Lambeth Council, was a year younger than Norma and was called John Major. A little dubious, Miss Bronhill told her to bring him round so that she could see him for herself.

Norma duly presented him for inspection at Harriet Walk. The moment Miss Bronhill saw John her mind was put at rest. 'I knew immediately that he would be the kind of man who would look after her,' she says. 'I thought he was very good-looking and quite charming, but, like her, a little sensitive. If it's not too much of a cliché, I'd say that they seemed made for each other.'

Her husband Richard Finny remembers that the couple just stood in the hall, peering nervously at him and his wife. He made a disastrous attempt at breaking the ice by asking John with a dead-pan face about his prospects. His guest coughed nervously and then embarked on a long, earnest monologue about his future at the Standard Chartered Bank. When the laid-back Australian started sniggering, John and Norma gazed at him with total bewilderment on their faces. 'Seeing them together like that, they just didn't seem quite real,' says Finny. 'If it'd been any other couple, I'd have thought they were parodying themselves.'

From a man who has seen as much of the world and its ways as Finny, it was not such a surprising response. Here was this shy, timid pair, looking for all the world as if they had just stepped out of one of those cosy, old-fashioned Bisto adverts, talking sensibly about marriage and settling down. The sixties had just happened – free love, Ban the Bomb and the Beatles – and John and Norma didn't appear to have noticed.

Norma had met John in one of the most socially acceptable ways possible: through a mutual friend. Peter Golds had got to know John very well through his work for the Conservatives and he unknowingly brought about the fateful meeting when he cajoled Norma into acting as a driver for the Greater London Council elections that spring, ferrying voters to the polling stations. At the end of a long, tiring day, she found herself standing in the committee rooms at the association's head-quarters at 332 Brixton Road, feeling a little out of place among the grey-suited party workers in her sleeveless check jacket, short skirt and blouse and long white leather boots.

John spotted her the moment he walked in. He discreetly asked Golds who she was. Golds smiled knowingly and introduced him to Norma Johnson. There was no time for a long conversation – John was *en route* to the count at the Town Hall – but Golds felt that there was an evident chemistry at that first encounter. 'You could tell, it was the way they looked at each other, the body language,' says Golds. 'I remember thinking these two would be seeing each other again before long.' Alicia Gains, who also saw them together, says: 'It was uncanny. When you know somebody very well, you sometimes know when someone is going to be right for them. I just knew that John was going to be right for Norma.'

Norma says that for *her* it was actually love at first sight. In the few minutes that they had spent talking, John, sporting sideboards and wearing a brown suit and his NHS glasses, impressed her as 'glamorous . . . gorgeous . . . kind . . . but a bit pushy, a bit bossy . . . And I rather liked the idea of him being on the council . . . councillors got invited to quite nice things.' Asked what he had thought of her at that first meeting, John was a shade more taciturn: 'I thought she was super. She had the biggest brown eyes I had ever seen.'

As he left, John told Golds to try and get Norma into the count, something he was able to arrange by calling in a few favours. For anybody with an interest in politics, it was a riveting evening, with the result on a knife edge. For Norma, it must have been a singularly tiring affair as several recounts were called and the proceedings dragged on until dawn. But she was rewarded for hanging on: she got to give her 'gorgeous' man a lift home in her Mini.

As they drove back through the deserted streets John was a little subdued, having just seen the Tories lose one of their four cherished seats at Lambeth. Norma made polite small-talk and, glancing at him occasionally as she drove along, she tried to think of a ruse that would ensure that their paths crossed again in the near future. As she dropped him off, she asked him, as casually as she could, if he would care to come to a dinner party she was holding later that week for a few friends. Of course she hadn't actually got a dinner party arranged, but she knew that she could get one together at short notice if need be. To her delight, he accepted the invitation.

The path of true love never running smoothly, he phoned at the last minute to cancel, saying that he had got a better offer: he had been offered a ticket to see a performance of *Elijah*. Norma, not especially fond of entertaining at the best of times, was left to soldier on through a pointless dinner party. But she did not give up. A few days later, she thought she would give it one last go and invited John to a production of *Aida*, but again, no luck. He said he had a prior engagement.

Norma understandably felt that she had been making all the running: 'I dated him,' she says, 'not the other way around.' At the age of twenty-eight, her eagerness to net John was perhaps understandable, but he was in fact every bit as keen, though he had been playing the game a shrewder way. He had turned down the dinner party because he reasoned that if Norma was hosting it, she would have had little, if any, opportunity to have a proper chat with him. As for the opera, he had, funnily enough, tried to get tickets to *Aida* himself so that he could invite her – he apparently considered this the correct way of doing things. 'I never told her that,' he says. 'I thought it was a good idea not to.'

John finally made his move by inviting Norma to come as his guest to a dinner which Lawrence Kennedy, an old friend of his on the council, was having at his home in Dulwich with his wife Aine. It was an occasion when John knew that he would be able to talk to Norma to his heart's content and things would be able to take their course. His instinct was spot on. Of that dinner, Norma comments: 'That was the first night I really got to know him. He was warm, funny and charming and I guess our romance started then.' She says she asked him three questions: did he wear braces, tank tops or ever carry a purse? To her relief, he answered 'no' to all of them. She wanted to be sure that she wasn't getting mixed up with another man like her first boyfriend.

John too realised that night had been a turning point. Not long afterwards, he wrote a letter to Bette Grainger, an Australian secretary whom he had been dating, and informed her that he had met someone 'very special' and therefore felt it best if they ended their relationship. He told her that, under the circumstances, he felt it would be best if they didn't see each other again. He hoped that she would understand. Bette refers to it jokingly as her '*from* John' letter, but, even though it was sensitively written, it hurt her a great deal. A vivacious girl with dark hair and brown eyes – she describes herself as similar to Norma, 'only bigger' – she had been going out with John for about six months, and had secretly wished that she might one day have become Mrs Major herself. Certainly it had been what a lot of their friends had been expecting.

With Bette dealt with, John put a not inconsiderable amount of effort into the job of courting Norma. Her name appeared in his diary on just about every evening that hadn't already been marked down for council business. The first occasion when they went out together on their own was for a gala evening at Covent Garden for Sir David Webster, the opera house's distinguished administrator. The evening was not a huge success. John made Norma aware that he found queuing an intensely irritating way of beginning a night out. Two late nights in the council chamber had made him tetchy, and later, as they took their seats, sleepy. At the very moment Norma's idol, Joan Sutherland, strode on to the stage to sing the mad scene from Donizetti's *Lucia di Lammermoor*, he nodded off. Thereafter Norma always picked up the tickets in advance and chose the productions with great care, though on one occasion she had to take him blind to *Die Meistersinger*. Just before the curtain went up, he told her, unpromisingly, that he was glad she had brought him along because he liked folk groups.

All those who knew John were amused by his overnight conversion to the recondite world of opera. Joy Murray, wife of John's council colleague Geoffrey, says: 'It was hilarious, it wasn't his scene at all.' John's elder sister, Mrs Pat Dessoy, diplomatically never told Norma that the only records he had ever collected before he had started going out with her had been the Hollies'. 'The moment I heard that John was sitting through opera for this girl, I realised it *had* to be serious,' she says.

Six weeks after their first meeting, Norma and John were engaged. Before making the announcement, John took Norma to see his mother, Gwen, who was in the Mayday Hospital in Croydon, suffering from emphysema. She had spent almost all of 1970 in hospital, and, John who loved his mother very dearly and has said his early life had revolved around her, knew that she had little time left. Mrs Dessoy was there when he brought Norma into her room. It was, she recalls, a moving encounter. 'Hospital visiting hours only extended to half an hour in those days, but a lot seemed to be said in a very short time. Mother was actually rather surprised that her youngest son had fallen in love so suddenly, but she was not unhappy about his choice. She most definitely approved of Norma.'

It was John's dearest wish that his mother should be able to attend his wedding, which had been set for 3 October. He had even engaged a nurse to look after her on the day. A month before, Mrs Major took a turn for the worse, and, since it was obvious that she wouldn't be well enough to go to the church, John said that he wanted to postpone the wedding until her condition improved. All too aware what the real situation was, Mrs Major was just as adamant that people should not be inconvenienced on her account. Just a few days later, she died.

Norma, along with Clive Jones, a good-humoured, portly friend of John's from the council, and Rose Oliphant, one of Mrs Major's neighbours, were the only non-family members at the service at the Variety Artists' Chapel at Streatham Vale Crematorium. She was laid to rest beside her husband Tom Major, a one-time music-hall performer. It was a cold, rainy day in September and Norma cried. It meant a lot to John that Norma was there. As Clive Jones says: 'His sister Pat and his brother Terry both had their spouses there to support them. Norma was there to support him and he needed her. The fact he had her with him on that day showed that he thought of her, even then, as a member of the family.'

Although Mrs Major's death inevitably cast a shadow over the event, John and Norma's wedding at St Matthew's Church, Brixton, went ahead as planned. On the day, there were all the traditional dramas, and a few new ones. In the morning, the bride discovered that three blobs of machine oil had somehow dripped on to her wedding dress. She ingeniously camouflaged them by attaching some strategically-positioned lace flowers. The groom's left knee, injured in a road accident a few years earlier, had been playing up and Clive Jones, the best man, was terrified that it would give way half-way up the aisle. 'I'd spent the night before in his flat with him and he wasn't in a terribly good state,' says Jones. 'I had visions of him collapsing on top of Norma.' Even the order of service had to be rearranged at the last minute because Miss Bronhill, who had been invited as a guest, had volunteered to perform, and she had hurriedly been put down to sing a solo of 'Ave Maria' while John and Norma went into the annex to sign the register. 'Norma didn't think that was fair,' Jones recalls with a grin. 'She wanted to be able to hear June sing too.'

As it was, the service went off without a hitch. Norma, who was given away by an uncle, discreetly supported her new husband as they walked out of the church. ('You'll have to carry *me* out,' John had whispered to her at the altar, only half in jest.) The dress won plaudits from everyone present. The reporter from the *South London Press* noted that it was of the bride's own design, and consisted of 'a bodice of guipure lace sewn with crystal drops merging in a velvet skirt and train'.

None of the groom's family appeared in the photographs taken on the steps outside the church on that unusually windy morning. The most senior member of Major's family at the service, Mrs Dessoy, was heavily pregnant and was more than happy to stay in the background. So the pictures showed just John and Norma, Clive Jones, three bridesmaids in their turquoise dresses

– also, incidentally, designed and made by Norma – and, all got up in pale pink and her blonde hair immaculately coiffed, the bride's mother, Mrs Johnson, with an umistakable look of triumph on her face. As Mrs Dessoy puts it: 'I couldn't help thinking that it was Edith's day almost as much as Norma's. It was the day she had got what she really wanted in life. John was precisely the sort of man she had wanted Norma to marry – a man with prospects.'

The reception was held at committee room 119 at Lambeth Town Hall, just across the road from the church. Jones remembers it was a somewhat unusual affair in two respects: instead of the bride and groom circulating among the guests, the guests had to circulate around the bride and groom because John was in so much pain that he had difficulty standing. Jones says that he was struck too by the fact that almost all of the guests were friends of John's – most of them, inevitably, councillors, party workers and others whom he had felt it politically expedient to invite. Even Pat Hellicar, the local government reporter from the *South London Press*, had been asked along. In his speech, John joked that the reason why he had asked virtually the entire council to his wedding was because Norma had thought it would make everyone aware that he was now a married man and maybe – just maybe – they might occasionally let him go home to her.

As the proceedings drew to a close, Mr and Mrs Major headed off for their honeymoon in Ibiza in their white Mini, a few empty baked bean cans clattering on strings behind them, the surreptitious work of one of John's fellow councillors, John Steel. The couple left in their wake a group of friends and relatives dazed by the extraordinary speed of events. Clive Jones says that he had hardly become acquainted with Norma before John had informed him he would be marrying her. 'It took me aback,' he admits. 'John had been seen on the council as a solid, conscientious fellow who liked plenty of time to arrive at any decision, let alone a decision of this magnitude.' None of John's friends was in any doubt that his relationship with Norma had developed into a strong and loving one, but one or two admit that they were not unaware that for him to get married at that point was helpful politically. As Geoffrey Murray, another Lambeth councillor who was a guest at the wedding, explains: 'He wanted to be an MP and he knew as well as anyone that selection committees liked candidates to be married.'

John himself uses the word 'calculating' to describe the way that he had set about making himself attractive to the selection committees which he knew he would be facing in the future: his council work, his job at the bank, his school governorship and his involvement with voluntary bodies had all served his purpose. Mr Murray's conjecture that to some extent John may have seen Norma as one additional asset does not therefore seem un-reasonable. Certainly Norma, a classic English rose, would clearly have gone down better with the selection committees than his Australian ex. The words John uses to describe how he decided to marry Norma don't exactly sound like those of a man head-over-heels in love: 'It was a couple of mornings after having met her. I was turning the thought over in my mind as I walked to catch the bus to work. It just became perfectly clear, I think.'

And John seemed to be thinking more like a politician than a young man in love when he decreed that the marriage had to fit in with the political calendar: it had to be either just before or just after that year's Conservative Party Conference. He even saw a picture opportunity on the wedding day itself, getting Pat Hellicar at the *South London Press* to send a photographer to take a picture of himself and his best man, Councillor Jones, making an official visit to a group of local tenants in top hat and tails, just before the service. As Jones points out, officials on the Housing Committee were actually extremely embarrassed when they discovered that they had inadvertently given their chairman a job on his wedding day, and would have been more than happy to have rescheduled it, but John saw a chance that was too good to be missed.

The story which appeared in the paper – headlined 'Bridegroom makes detour in tails' – was the sort that every politician loves to have written about him. It stated that Councillor Major and Councillor Jones had had no alternative but to squeeze in the visit a few hours before the service and quoted the dutiful bridegroom as saying: 'The only way we could save time was not to have to go home again and change for the wedding.' The piece was accompanied by a picture of the two incongruously dressed councillors surrounded by a group of grumpy-looking tenants who obviously hadn't seen the funny side of the situation.

It is easy to see parallels between the young John Major and Leslie Titmuss, John Mortimer's repulsively ambitious Tory politician in *Paradise Postponed*, but John must have had his redeeming features to have won the respect of so many people around him, not least the members of his own family. 'We all knew that John was going places,' says his brother, Terry Major-Ball. 'We knew he would leave us all behind, but we just thought "Good luck to him. He deserves it."' Without a hint of bitterness in her voice, Mrs Pat Dessoy, his sister, remarks: 'John needed a lifestyle in which he would get to know the sort of people who would help him get to where he wanted to go. I realised that I had to let go of him.'

Outside the council chamber, when he wasn't hiding behind his desk and his charcoal grey suit and talking in the cold, impenetrable language of the official minutes, there was in fact an endearing vulnerability about John. He was a little awkward, unsure of himself socially, desperately seeking and needing approval, and a little over-sensitive, perhaps because, like Norma, he had had no real paternal influence in his life.

If there was little doubt that Norma was inexperienced in love, there is a consensus among John's friends and relatives that he too was a virgin when he walked up the aisle with Norma at the age of twenty-seven. A long-time political ally, Jean Lucas, says that John had dated a number of girls before Norma, not just Bette Grainger, but also a publican's daughter who had a flat on Burton Road, Brixton, but she knew that he would have been aghast at the idea of going to bed with any of them. Ms Grainger bears this out: 'John had *views* on sex before marriage, and, I might add, I did as well. All our relationship entailed was seeing each other once or twice a week. We'd watch the telly at his flat, visit the cinema, take walks, see Chelsea play at home, that sort of thing.'

John's brother, Terry Major-Ball, says that their mother had inculcated in both of them 'strict rules about girls, about how they were to be treated. They were to be treated as *ladies*.' Asked if she believed John had been a virgin when he married, Pat Dessoy was moved to make a strikingly eloquent statement: 'We Majors don't believe in sexual promiscuity. We have old-fashioned values: honesty, your country, your family, an obligation to a higher authority yet. We don't go around preaching, we quietly go ahead and live our lives the way that we feel is right.'

All of this of course is what made John so right for his bride. There had been a man in her life before him, whom she had alluded to vaguely on occasions but found it difficult to talk about because it had ended badly. 'I heard his name mentioned from time to time,' says Stella Brown (née Matthews), her friend from Bourn. 'Then suddenly I never heard his name again. Norma did not talk about what happened, and I felt it best not to ask.' A shy, gentle girl, Norma had never been attracted by machismo, and, indeed, a great many of the young men whom she had met and befriended through her regular visits to the opera happened to be homosexuals. Ian Cameron Black, a colleague of John's at the bank who became a close friend of Norma's, referred to them as 'the pretty boys', while Mrs Dessoy's preferred euphemism is 'young men who were rather ahead of their time'.

Mrs Dessoy reckons that Norma could initially have been a little naive about 'things like that' – she had, after all, spent a sizeable chunk of her life in girls' boarding-schools – but once the situation had become clear to her, she saw no reason why she should treat any of these men differently, even though, Mrs Dessoy says, her mother made little secret of the fact that she had disapproved of them. Mrs Dessoy considers this very typical of Norma: 'A lot of people go around looking for reasons why they can't be friendly with people. Norma has never been like that. She is always looking for reasons why she *can* like people.'

Norma's friend Alicia Gains says: 'If you go to somewhere like Covent Garden regularly, you find a certain percentage of the audience is going to be gay. There are some people of course who don't like them because of their sexuality, but as far as we were concerned that was not any of our business. What they did in their own time was their concern. We just liked them as people. We accepted them for what they were, and we found that they were charming, witty and great fun to be with.'

Like Olly Dowden in Thomas Hardy's *Return of the Native*, Norma was a woman who just seemed to go about her daily routine 'grateful to all the world for letting her remain alive'. Her friend Stella Brown says that she was struck by the way that she didn't lose any enthusiasm for having her to stay even as she moved into sophisticated new circles in London. 'I had a very strong Cambridge accent and real country manners and country ways during my teens,' she recalls. 'I think that a lot of upwardly mobile Londoners might have been ashamed of knowing someone like that, but not Norma. She happily introduced me to everybody, even after I became a Socialist.'

John says that Norma is a woman with no guile at all. He rather liked that, but some of his friends wondered if her warm nature, unusual sensitivity and unworldliness meant that she was really cut out to be a politician's wife. Barbara Wallis, a colleague of John's on the council, sat down with her a few days before the engagement to talk to her about what it would be like. 'What you will want more than anything will be time with John, but as his career progresses – and progress it will very soon – you must understand that you will have less and less of it . . . ' Norma replied that this was something that she had already come to terms with. Looking Barbara straight in the eyes, she declared: 'John's happiness takes priority over everything else in my life. If politics is what matters to him, then I will do everything I can to support him.'

As for the kind of woman John wanted Norma to be, there is a clue perhaps in his disclosure that his favourite literary heroine is Lily Dale from Anthony Trollope's *The Small House at Allington*. Lily just muddles through as best she can in a difficult world, forever true to her own ideals and values, however impractical, masochistic or foolishly romantic they may seem to others. Happiness for Lily is simply the love of a good man. She wants only to look up into her man's eyes and declare herself 'your own, to take when you please, and to leave untaken while you please'.

Very frequently, as it happened, did it please John to leave Norma untaken. In the early days of their marriage he would often telephone home to say that some crisis or other at the council was detaining him. A great many lovingly prepared meals went uneaten. When he did eventually get home, he would usually be so tired that all he wanted to do was sleep. Bernard Perkins, the leader of the council and a man whose own marriage failed because he put politics first on too many occasions, felt for Norma. 'It could not have been easy for her,' he says. 'She was young and she had just begun a new life with a man whom she loved – and yet she was hardly allowed to spend any time with him. I am sure that she knew it was going to be difficult, but I doubt if she could have realised how difficult. John put in the most extraordinarily long hours at the council.'

There was however little sympathy to be had elsewhere for Norma. Her friend Peter Golds says simply that she had known what she had been letting herself in for. Her own mother had of course had far more to contend with at her age, so Norma couldn't go crying on her shoulder. As for her in-laws, Mrs

Dessoy notes: 'When you are married, you support your husband. It doesn't matter whether that means you have to adapt or put up with things that you don't like. You put up with it.'

Norma was very affected by Bernard and Pat Perkins' divorce. It brought home to her quite how fragile a political marriage could be. Pat remembers Norma telling her: 'At least I had an idea about what I was getting myself into when I married John. When you married Bernard, you hadn't any inkling that he might go into politics.'

The social obligations of being a councillor's wife weighed heavily on Norma and she often turned to Pat for advice about facing up to the big functions they used to have in the leader's parlour. 'She asked me once how I kept so cool walking beside my husband into rooms full of strangers,' says Pat. 'I told her I felt physically sick but I had learnt how to hide it with a smile.'

The role would of course have been so much easier for Norma if she had been interested in politics, but, try as she might, she could never work up any enthusiasm for the affairs of Lambeth Council. Barbara Wallis remembers Norma coming round to her flat with John and a few other councillors after a committee meeting. They all went into the dining room and talked politics while Norma, very characteristically, disappeared upstairs to watch Keith Michell – a favourite actor of hers since *Robert and Elizabeth* – in *The Six Wives of Henry VIII*. Margaret Marshall, another political ally of John's, observes wryly: 'Politics was never the be-all and end-all for Norma as it had been for the rest of us. Maybe she suffered from a maturity that the rest of us didn't have.'

Even if Norma had been eager to listen to her husband on the agonies and ecstasies of chairing a local housing committee, he was not inclined to talk. 'John soon saw that it made sense to keep his life as a politician separate from his life as a family man,' says Peter Golds. 'He drew a line between his roles as a politician and a husband.' John confided in Alicia Gains that it was his ambition to hold down one of the great offices of state, but he never told Norma that. Barbara Wallis speaks of John 'compartmentalising' his life, keeping each compartment sealed off from the others so that nobody could ever see the whole picture. The man Norma knew as her husband was not therefore the man that his friend Ian Cameron Black had known as a colleague at the bank, or Bernard Perkins had known as a councillor. To be sure, it struck Cameron Black as strange how people would come and talk about close friends of John whose names he had never heard mentioned in the twenty-five years he had known him. (The television journalist Michael Crick, who interviewed innumerable friends of John for a *Panorama* profile, jokes that he would have liked to have got them all together in one room and asked them if they knew who it was that they had in common. He doubted very much if any of them would, coming from such a cross-section of society.)

Margaret Marshall, a local Conservative activist, says it was obvious that Norma had found herself in a situation that was far from perfect, but she was impressed by the fact she never complained. 'That was not her way – instead she just kept herself busy: doing her dressmaking jobs; methodically preparing meals, freezing them, keeping the flat clean, and generally getting things organised, so that John would be able to relax when he got home. And then of course when John had council meetings, she always had the opera to go to.'

The first big decision that the Majors had to make as a couple was where to live. Norma naturally preferred her own flat at Anerley Park to her husband's sparsely furnished bachelor pad in Primrose Court. The dilemma was finally decided, as so many things were, on political grounds. As a councillor in Lambeth, John felt it advantageous to continue living in the area, so Primrose Court it was. Conditions there were not quite as basic as has been made out. Peter Golds could not remember, for example, the famous tallboys covered in Formica which served as a dining-room table. 'Actually Norma brought along some pretty classy furniture with her from Anerley Park,' he points out. 'She made it very habitable.' That is not to say that they were well-off. Norma, like her mother before her, had to get by on a very tight budget. Her housekeeping allowance from John was a frugal £8-a-week. Her skills as a dressmaker – and even a shirt- and bow-tie-maker for John – helped her keep her outgoings down, and for a time she took a job as a supply teacher at Norwood School to bring in some extra cash. However, she had to give that up when she started suffering from backache, stomachache and sickness. She went to the doctor and discovered that she was pregnant. After he had discovered, John bought her a bottle of her favourite perfume, Carven Magriffe, by way of thanks.

Norma knew very well that Primrose Court was no place for bringing up a baby. It had been perfectly adequate for one, a little confined for two, but it would be decidedly cramped when the third member of the family arrived. Just as Norma was wondering how on earth she was going to get by, somebody else moved in. John decided that John Steel, a fellow councillor, needed to be among friends as he recovered from a horrific road accident that had killed his wife, Jennifer. John Steel used to be a neighbour at Primrose Court, but, just before the accident, he had sold his flat to set up home in Burgess Hill with Jennifer, whom he had married only months before the crash. John and Norma were among the first of his friends to visit him at Cuckfield Hospital, and, seeing that he obviously didn't relish the idea of having to go to an unfamiliar neighbourhood when he was discharged, John had asked him if he would like to move in with them. 'You can stay as long as you like,' John told him. Norma nodded her head in agreement. Steel gratefully accepted their invitation.

Norma welcomed Steel very warmly and went out of her way to make him feel at home. Left in the flat together most days, they got to know each other well. Steel confided in her that he had fallen in love with a nurse at the hospital whom he wanted to marry. He could tell that Norma didn't think it a good idea for him to throw himself into another relationship quite so quickly, but she never lectured him. 'That is what made it such a pleasure to be with her – she never presumed to tell anyone what to do,' says Steel. 'She communicated what she thought by the expressions on her face.'

John he saw only fleetingly – he always seemed to be rushing out to get to some meeting. On the rare occasions that he did have time on his hands he would settle down in his armchair and read political biographies. Steel thinks that he read them as if they were training manuals. Not long after Steel moved in, Norma's baby was born – it had been Steel who got up, in some pain, and drove her to the hospital. The Majors touchingly named their baby Elizabeth Jennifer after Steel's late wife and made him a godfather. It took a while for Steel to make a full recovery, and, as his stay dragged on for several months, the pressure inevitably began to take its toll on Norma, especially after she had started taking on commissions to do some freelance dressmaking work. It was a pretty chaotic existence: there was material all over the place, John always on the move, Steel stretched out on the sofa, and, more often than not, the baby crying. In the kitchen with John one evening, Norma found the teat of Elizabeth's milk bottle blocked, and, after several sleepless nights, she finally snapped and hurled it at the wall. John set to and together they cleaned up the carpet and wiped the mess off the wall. By the time they had finished, Elizabeth was sleeping soundly.

Margaret Marshall accepts that it had not been an isolated incident. 'John and Norma often had what you could describe as a lively exchange of views, but I think that was quite understandable in the circumstances,' she says. 'I heard them arguing myself from time to time, but I never came away thinking that there was any instability in the marriage.' To their neighbours, the Majors certainly always seemed to epitomise suburban respectability, if not actually dreariness. A couple called the Bartletts, who lived in the flat opposite, say that their most interesting memory of them was the time that Norma had a breakdown. It took her some hours, apparently, before she could get her Mini going again.

Norma remained a councillor's wife for less than a year. John, who had won his seat in the 1968 Conservative landslide, was aware that the local government elections in 1971 were going to be difficult, coming as they did when Edward Heath was encountering the inevitable mid-term problems. John abandoned his own ward, Ferndale, for Clapham Park, which seemed a slightly better bet. It made little difference – he still went down with everyone else and the Socialists regained Lambeth. Peter Golds remembers that Norma was 'devastated', not of course for herself, but for her husband, because she knew how important it had been to him.

Norma might not have realised it, but this was not the end for John; it was the beginning. Instead of plotting a comeback in Lambeth, he decided that it was as good a time as any to launch himself on his parliamentary career. He received the reply he had hoped for when he asked one Tory agent: 'Could somebody like me hope to get on to the Candidates' List?' Within a year, he was adopted as the prospective Conservative Party candidate for Camden, St Pancras North. It was a hopeless cause, but considered by Conservative Central Office to be as good a place as any for him to cut his teeth. Norma did not herself campaign in the election in 1974, having one or two other matters to attend to. The family was moving to a new, more spacious house on the West Oak estate in Beckenham, there was Elizabeth to look after, and she also happened to be pregnant again.

Norma knew very well what her husband's chances were. She certainly did not see herself as a future MP's wife. Margaret Marshall, who was a prospective parliamentary candidate for more constituencies than she cares to remember, says Norma used to be dumbfounded by the way young political aspirants would keep banging their heads against brick walls. 'I remember coming in once and telling her that I had got selected to fight some new seat and Norma sighed and said, "Oh, no, Margaret, not again . . . "" The hopelessness of the campaign at St Pancras North even left John with doubts. Margaret Jay, his agent, remembers him turning to her at one point and asking: 'Do you think I am doing the right thing? Am I being fair to my wife and family to give up a secure job at the bank for all this?' Margaret looked at him and replied: 'Politics is in your blood, John. You're never going to be happy until you have had a go at it.'

There must also have been growing doubts in John's mind about whether Norma really would be happy as an MP's wife. He had become aware that in the Conservative Party a great deal is expected of the wives, not least as public performers. One incident in particular at about this time must have made him realise quite how much his wife detested being the centre of attention. He had gone with Norma to the Coliseum to see June Bronhill in concert. It was a full house and they were sitting in the front row of the dress circle with their friend Ian Cameron Black. Suddenly in the middle of the performance Miss Bronhill noticed Norma and waved at her from the stage. 'Hello, Norma, how are both of you?' she asked. The entire audience turned and looked at Norma which made her very flustered. She didn't know what to say or do. Cameron Black feels that Miss Bronhill's use of the word 'both' had been particularly unfortunate because Norma was at the time very obviously pregnant. Miss Bronhill sensed Norma's discomfort and tried to regain her audience's attention by showing off the dress she was wearing and announcing it was one that Norma had made for her. Anyone else might have laughed it off, but not Norma. She hated everybody looking at her.

Norma was happiest in the bosom of her family. The two-up, two-down that John had bought in Beckenham must have seemed very much more like a home to her than Primrose Court. After James was born in 1975, her life revolved around the family. The house backed on to a large communal field which was ideal for the children to play in. David Rogers, a neighbour, remembers how Norma used to make miniature theatres from a variety of household items in true *Blue Peter* style. The children would then put on their own productions with little home-made characters that they attached to sticks. John would be home every weekend and he and Norma had a cosy little ritual of watching *The Onedin Line* on BBC 1 on Sunday nights as they ate their dinner off trays.

There were still a lot of selection committees to face, but Norma was becoming accustomed to them, seeing them as a kind of occupational hazard. John's friend Robert Atkins, in those days another local politician with parliamentary ambitions, says Norma confided in him how toffee-nosed she found some of them. She was astounded when the chairman of a selection committee on the south coast actually asked her to stand up and turn round so that he could see what she looked like from behind. It was so terribly sexist: the committees never even bothered to ask to see the husbands of female applicants, let alone look at their bottoms.

Norma had plenty of time too for her friends in those days. She delighted Ian Cameron Black and Peter Golds by making them James's godfathers. Clive Jones remembers eyebrows being raised at the announcement because Golds was Jewish, though he was not practising. 'A lot of people would have had a problem with that, but not Norma,' says Jones. 'She knew he would make a terrific godfather and she didn't care what anybody thought.' When Margaret Marshall had an accident while campaigning in the 1974 election that left her with problems getting up and down the stairs to her flat, Norma unhesitatingly suggested she should come and stay with them. 'They made me feel at home,' Miss Marshall says. 'It was a tremendously happy little household.'

Then one morning a letter landed on the doormat. Norma took it up to John with the breakfast and she was with him in the bed when he opened it. 'Oh, I've got an interview for Huntingdon,' he said matter-of-factly. He had been a bit miserable after having made no progress in a succession of seats and hadn't even bothered to tell Norma he had put in for it. It was after all a huntin', fishin' and shootin' environment, hardly his natural milieu, and he couldn't have had less in common with its retiring Member, Sir David Renton, an old Tory of the Dreadnought Class.

Huntingdon seemed to capture Norma's imagination. She knew the area well, having lived briefly in the nearby village of Bourn during the war years. Her father's family had roots in the area, too. She sensed the hand of fate: maybe this really was going to be the one. On one point she was quite clear, however: no matter what happened in John's career, she would be staying put. Her friend and neighbour from Primrose Court, Joy Murray, remembers that she was quite adamant about that. 'You see, Joy, all my friends are here,' she had told her. 'There is no worthwhile opera outside of London, and you know I couldn't possibly survive without that.'

CHAPTER 3

The Woman in Red

SHORTLY AFTER John Major was chosen to contest Sir David Renton's seat for the Conservatives in 1976, Norma and the children moved with him to their new home in Hemingford Grey, a village five miles from Huntingdon on the Cambridge Road. Her regular visits to the London opera houses were to be the first of many sacrifices.

Norma's debut in the constituency had been inauspicious to say the least. At Shire Hall, where the local Conservative Party Association met to adopt Sir David's successor, she walked in wearing a bright red dress. There was a lot of tut-tutting among the supporters of some of her husband's top-drawer rivals such as the Marquis of Douro, a descendant of the Duke of Wellington, and the avuncular Mr Jock Bruce-Gardyne (ex-Royal Dragoons), who saw it as further proof that the 'bank clerk' – as some of them contemptuously called John – and his 'mousey little wife' simply weren't up to the job.

To others, such as Emily Blatch, a local party activist, the dress proved to be rather endearing: 'Norma was very obviously not a typical politician's wife and I found that refreshing,' she recalls. 'There was none of the hardness or the pushiness that one had come to expect of a politician's wife. This woman wasn't trying to score points or compete with anyone.' Indeed, she even crossed the floor to have a word with Sarah Bruce-Gardyne, the wife of her husband's rival. 'She was extremely nice and friendly,' says Sarah. 'These sort of occasions are usually pretty horrible, and, having just come out of hospital the day before, I wasn't feeling 100 per cent, but Mrs Major rather cheered me up. One usually felt a need to hold oneself back a bit at these meetings and be a bit on one's guard, but Mrs Major made it all seem rather warmer and rather more congenial than it might otherwise have been. After chatting to her, one felt it very difficult to think of her as a rival at all.'

Norma won another admirer at that meeting in no less a personage than Sir David himself. The old man becomes almost misty-eyed when he speaks about the moment he first set eyes upon her: 'When I saw John standing there with her, I thought, by Jove, he's a lucky fellow. What a pretty wife he has. I had a short chat with them, but Norma didn't speak much unless spoken to. She was shy, modest and charming.'

After John had said his piece to the committee, he took Norma out to a nearby pub for a quick drink: a tomato juice for him, an orange juice for her. Neither felt that it was an occasion for alcohol. Then as they walked out, John noticed a woman running towards them shouting excitedly. He turned to Norma and said with typical understatement: 'I think we've won.' She had been used to consoling him at moments like this. Her husband actually winning was the last thing she had expected and she simply didn't know what to say.

John hadn't prepared her for victory any more than he had prepared himself. He had told Ian Cameron Black that he was reconciled to the fact that the association almost certainly wouldn't want somebody representing them who had grown up 'on the wrong side of the Thames'. And that had been not only *his* view of his chances. Crossbencher, writing with his customary prescience in the *Sunday Express* the week before, had noted that it was a two-horse race between Douro and Bruce-Gardyne.

As they walked back towards Shire Hall, the Majors' astonishment gave way to apprehension at the formidable job of work that lay ahead. Sir David noted that they were not a couple 'who appeared to have much experience of rural life' – a polite euphemism in those parts for 'townies' – and added that it was clear to him they were both going to need all the help that they could get. Sir David, once described by Sir Alec Douglas-Home as 'a model Parliamentarian', resolved to do everything he could to ensure that they both made 'all the right connections'. After the adoption meeting, he invited them to stay the weekend with him and his wife Paddy at the Moat House, the family's imposing 500-year-old country residence at Abbots Ripton, just outside Huntingdon.

It is hard to imagine two couples with less in common than the Rentons and the Majors. The former looked and sounded as if they had stepped straight out of an Evelyn Waugh novel, the latter from something by Alan Bennett. As Olive Baddeley, an official of the local Conservative Association, puts it: 'They came from different classes.' In the event, they all got on surprisingly well. Sir David, a pernickety character who, as the Recorder at Guildford Petty Sessions, once famously ordered a juryman to step down for turning up dressed in a boilersuit, found John a pleasing and eager student. To his relief, the young man did not give him any trenchant lectures about how he had pulled himself up by his bootstraps, but instead listened respectfully as he showed him around the constituency, introducing him to a seemingly endless procession of local worthies. It wasn't long before Sir David concluded that John would have no problems at all taking over from him. He didn't think that he was exactly the sort of fellow who would make the premiership, but, with a fair wind behind him, he had the makings of a first-rate constituency MP. (If there had been one thing about John Major which had been a disappointment to Sir David, it was that he didn't ride. 'It was such a help in getting oneself seen in the constituency,' Sir

David observes wistfully. 'I used to think that it was enough sometimes just to be seen riding through villages on my horse.')

Of Norma's ability to step into his wife's elegant high-heels, Sir David was considerably less confident: 'To be perfectly honest, Norma seemed a bit puzzled at first by what was required of her in the constituency. She did not take to it easily. I doubted then if she had much interest in politics. She seldom accompanied John and I to meet the branch supporters. Her principal concern appeared to be her children.' Norma knew that even though she did have a good two years to rehearse before the General Election, she had a very hard act to follow in Lady Renton. Attractive, well-educated, and a great society figure in her day, Paddy Renton was a tireless speaker at civic gatherings, starter of egg-and-spoon races and opener of garden fêtes. As Sir David says: 'My wife told me, "You never proposed to me, David. You just asked if I would mind opening a fête."'

The organisations with which she was connected covered the length and breadth of the sprawling ninety-square-mile constituency and beyond, and would have filled up almost as much space as her husband's entry in *Who's Who*. She chaired both the constituency women's and entertainments committees and presided over Huntingdon Red Cross. She also worked for innumerable charities helping the disabled, following the birth of her own mentally handicapped daughter. She chaired Demand, Design and Manufacture for Disability and was president of the Greater London Association for Disabled People. She also saw herself very much as her husband's partner, inclined to argue with him on matters of government policy – politically she was to the right of her husband, which was very right indeed – and she would even sit in on newspaper interviews he gave and interject comments of her own. On weekdays she went up to London with her husband and stayed with him at their flat in Westminster. All her husband's interests, she said, were her interests.

It is hard to imagine a woman more unlike Lady Renton than Norma Major, but Her Ladyship still believed that she could mould her into her image. She suggested to her that she might care to 'shadow' her as she went about her duties in the constituency, in the same way that John was shadowing her husband. Norma watched in awe as she swept majestically through the constituency, taking the chair at her innumerable committees, speaking from the platforms of local charities, fielding questions at luncheons, attending to her correspondence, sorting out her husband's diary. And never a hair of her elegant coiffure out of place. Andrew Thomson, invidiously playing the part of Sir David's agent and John's agent-in-waiting, was privately opposed to Norma trailing around after Lady Renton, but, in the circumstances, thought it best to keep his own counsel. 'Norma would look at me after watching Paddy sometimes and say, "Oh God, Andrew, I can't do that,"' he recalls. 'I really do think it made it tougher for her spending so much time with Paddy. She ought to have been allowed to have come to terms with her position in her own way, in her own time, without being made to feel that she had to emulate anyone, let alone someone as accomplished as Paddy.'

Thomson suspected that as John had traversed the country looking for a seat, Norma had never really thought through what it would actually mean to be the wife of an MP. Having to move house, find new schools for the children, and suddenly start appearing at constituency functions were none of them things that she appeared to have prepared herself for, and, at the beginning, it all seemed to be a matter of, at best, crisis management. 'She would say to me sometimes that all she had wanted was a straightforward life,' Thomson says. 'And I used to reply, "If you wanted a straightforward life, dear, you should not have got involved with John."' The impression Thomson got was that Norma had very little sense of her own identity when she first arrived in the constituency. 'I think it was when she came to Huntingdon that she realised, perhaps reluctantly, that she had to be someone in her own right,' he says. 'It wasn't enough just to be John's wife.'

It is a very perceptive remark, considering Norma's life up until that point. The early years she had spent being shunted from one boarding-school to another, ending up finally at a vast monolithic state school. Always she was led, never, even after she was made head girl at Peckham, did she seem to lead. To her classmates, she was just a face in the crowd. She made little or no impression on anybody. She went into teaching because that was what most of the other girls in her class had wanted to do. It hadn't occurred to her to ask herself whether or not she would actually enjoy it, and, as it turned out, she didn't, yet she soldiered on for five years, and then threw it all away, without a second thought, to become a nanny. Her neighbours in Penge remembered that most evenings she stayed at home with her mother, even when she was well into her twenties, living her life, if a life it was at all, through flamboyant opera stars, just another face out there in the darkness of a huge auditorium.

Thomson, a bluff, warm-hearted Scotsman, took on the task of trying to bring Norma out of herself. He knew very well that if he failed she could easily fall prey to the county set, still circling like vultures after John's adoption, waiting, yearning, for the moment when they could turn round and say, 'We told you so – look at her, the silly little woman simply can't cope.' As Thomson says: 'They were being judged, both of them, wherever they went, all the time. I would go to the odd Sunday sherry morning with the Majors and the Rentons and I would see people looking at the two couples, sizing them up, making their comparisons. A lot of them had known David and Paddy for thirty years and they just didn't know what to make of John and Norma. What could they talk to them about? They didn't have a horse, a child at one of the great public schools, Norma didn't chair any local committees and John didn't have expert knowledge in constitutional law, or even a knighthood.'

One of the big problems with Norma, Thomson discovered, was that she could not muster the courage to speak in public, a feat that her predecessor had managed frequently, effortlessly and magnificently, and the constituents had rather come to expect it of the Member's wife. Emily Blatch, who swiftly became a family friend, tried to persuade Norma to accept an early invitation to speak to the US servicemen's wives' group at RAF Alconbury. She says: 'I remember saying to Norma that the wives really couldn't be more informal, that there was nothing in the least bit nerve-racking about it, and that she should just go along and do it. But she simply folded in on herself and I realised it was a hopeless cause.' Norma hated the idea of public speaking. She says that she had 'a fear of not being thought bright enough, of not coming up to people's expectations'.

It was hard enough to get Norma to go to constituency functions simply as a guest. She detested the way people used to look at her and all too often she would overhear dispiriting remarks like 'So *that*'s the new MP's wife . . . my goodness, she's nothing like Paddy Renton, is she?' Sometimes she would tremble visibly before she entered even the smallest gathering. 'I'd never come across a woman so shy and so unsure of herself,' says one stalwart of the local association. 'She couldn't even cope with people coming up to her and just saying "Hello, Mrs Major". She would start stammering and looking around her frantically like some sort of cornered animal. The great majority of us were all on her side, rooting for her, but I think it just took her a while to realise it.' Even the simplest public utterances – 'I declare this public library open' – were beyond Norma. It wasn't saying the words which she found so hard to cope with; it was the thought of all those people looking at her as she said them.

Even with a silent wife, John managed to increase the Conservative majority by 12,319 to 21,563, a clear indication that a new order had prevailed in Huntingdonshire. As he wrestled with problems such as stubble-burning, low-flying aircraft and Cruise missiles – all uppermost in his constituents' minds – his wife timidly felt her way into her role, still counting on Lady Renton for advice and moral support. It took Norma a while to start getting herself mentioned in the local newspaper, the *Cambridge Evening News*, even in passing. Looking through their cuttings files, it seems as if she did next to nothing during her husband's first few years. By contrast, Lady Renton, pressing on with her good works in the constituency, was still popping up all over the place, to the extent that a lot of constituents could have been forgiven for thinking that she was still the local MP's wife. Thomson was aware of this but says that he had decided against trying to raise Norma's profile by putting her forward for interviews with the local papers because she simply wasn't up to it; even the most sympathetic, undemanding women's page feature would have been an ordeal for her.

Thomson nurtured her very carefully in the early years. 'I used to say to her, "I am preparing you for when your times comes" and she used to reply, "Well, Andrew, it's not going to come for a while yet."' He was relieved that John was not thought of as a rising star by Fleet Street, as some of the other new boys at Westminster had been, because it meant that outsiders didn't keep ringing. Thomson says: 'If there had been any big-shot media people phoning between 1976 and '80 and got her, it would have been a disaster. She would have said "No, no, it's not me you want, it's John," and she would just have gone burbling away that she didn't know what to say, and they would have to wait until her husband got back, and, of course, it would have given a very bad impression.' Norma hated the phone. She never used it herself and saw it as an invasion of her privacy. Friends such as Dulcie Atkins, the wife of Robert Atkins, John's parliamentary colleague whom he had known since his days in Lambeth, used to think it odd that Norma never phoned her, but she soon realised that it was the phone, not her, that she didn't like. If Mrs Atkins wanted to speak to Norma, *she* had to phone *her*. At the house at Hemingford Grey, John had a telephone put in one of the back rooms specifically for political calls and Norma avoided it like the plague.

Norma had a support group of sorts in a small band of level-headed Conservative matriarchs who sensed her vulnerability and befriended her. They were Olive Baddeley, Maggie Scott, Sue Winn and Rosemary Juggins, all of whom were there for her, consoling, protecting and encouraging her. 'I think it is true to say that we all worried about Norma in the early days,' says Mrs Winn, a doughty old Tory warrior whose late husband fought in the Battle of Britain. 'She was quite happy with her lot, raising her family and running the house, and all of the extra risks that had suddenly been thrown at her came as a bit of a shock.' Mrs Juggins chips in: 'We felt protective towards her. We wanted to ease her way without pushing her.'

They were tremendous, those ladies, and Norma evidently appreciated their help. When she walked into a room full of strangers, she would look around for a familiar face, and there was a palpable sense of relief when she saw that Mrs Winn or Mrs Juggins or Mrs Scott was there too. She would immediately walk up and talk to them, and stay close, often ignoring requests to mingle. As much as Norma seemed to count on them, all the women still sensed a reserve in her, a final barrier around her that they were not to breach. None of them claims to be a real, deep friend of hers, but then Norma only had room for one of those in her life – and that was her husband. 'The moment I saw John and Norma together I was struck by what a loving and close couple they were,' says Mrs Juggins. 'They always seemed to be holding hands, and John used to call her Normy. [His other nickname for her, less flatteringly, was 'Grub'.] As to whether they did have any really close friends, I would not presume to say, but none of them could possibly be as important to them as each other.'

A few years after John's election, Andrew Thomson began to feel more confident about pushing Norma harder. 'I started saying to her, "Look, Norma, I don't want you to make a speech, I just want you to say a few words." "How about this?" she

51

would say. And we would talk it through. It was a long, drawn-out process, and if she ever thought that she could get out of doing something she would, but it was progress.' The list of local organisations that Norma was connected with started to build up: there was the opera group, the St Ives Players, a society of bell-ringers, Meals on Wheels, the WRVS, and of course the local Tory branches for whom she organised, among other things, a constituency version of *Mastermind*, an event which she took very seriously indeed as she traipsed around the various branches in her capacity as quizmaster. Having been so nervous in the past, it surprised people that she was prepared to take on a task in which she would be the centre of attention. But she could hide behind this role, and, with a list of correct answers in front of her, she didn't have to worry about what to say, or being made to look a fool.

Norma also took an active interest in Mencap and it was, a number of her friends testify, a revelation to see her with the mentally handicapped. There was none of the reserve or stand-offishness that so many people often unconsciously display. With the children, she would get down on her hands and knees, look directly into their eyes, and communicate with them in a way in which few people were able. 'It was very moving to see her with them,' says Barbara Wallis, John's constituency secretary. 'She brought out the very best in the children. It was a gift.' Fred Heddell, the charity's chief executive, was also impressed when he saw Norma with a group of mentally-handicapped adults. 'They came up and held her hand and put their arms around her,' he says. 'Mentally handicapped adults are not always the nicest people to do that to you, but she coped with it very well. I wouldn't say that she enjoyed it, but she certainly never gave the impression that she was not enjoying it. For someone who is quite shy and nervous herself, she is very good at putting them at their ease.'

Norma's involvement with Mencap was a particular source of pleasure to Sir David Renton. 'She never told me why she became involved, but I like to think that her interest in it was partly stimulated by the involvement of my wife and I and the fact that we have a severely handicapped daughter ourselves,' he says. Norma chaired committees for Mencap and led very much by example. She raised £5,000 in sponsorship by doing a marathon – something she trained for assiduously by pounding around the constituency with James whenever she got the chance. She boosted the local branch's coffers by a further £1,000 by organising sales of Christmas cards. Elizabeth Dix, the chairwoman of the local branch, considers her a tireless worker. 'When she joined us she said she wanted to be rather more than just a name on a letterhead,' she says. 'She was as good as her word. She has been worth her weight in gold to us.'

Norma soon came to the attention of Mencap's chairman, the former Whitehall *farceur*, Sir Brian Rix, who attended the local branch's ball, which was held in a marquee in Huntingdon. 'I could see that she was working very hard indeed, but all of it behind-the-scenes work, concerned only with the local set-up and not the national one,' says Rix. 'A lot of people who get involved in charity work seem to want the maximum amount of exposure for the minimum amount of effort – she seemed to want exactly the opposite. I was all the more impressed because she herself had no mentally-handicapped people in her own family. David Renton and I both have mentally-handicapped daughters so we obviously have an axe to grind, but Norma was doing it purely of her own volition. I thought that was rather marvellous.'

As a constituency wife, Norma was beginning to bear comparison to just about any of the wives of her husband's colleagues at Westminster. Andrew Thomson was at once delighted and relieved to see her come out and embrace the constituency with such enthusiasm – it paid dividends for John politically, and, as he was only too well aware, it was profoundly good for Norma in terms of her personal well-being. A lot of MPs' wives are never able to adapt to the new lifestyle, clinging hopelessly to the idea of a normal routine and a husband who will be back in the evenings in time for tea. Such women invariably become consumed by bitterness, frequently turn to the bottle, make their own lives and the lives of their children miserable and, all too often, set themselves on an inexorable course for the divorce courts.

Edna Healey, one of the most respected of the Westminster wives, says the choice for any woman married to an MP is stark: 'Either she keeps on waiting for her husband to get home, and goes quietly mad, or finds some interests of her own.' She adds that it might seem unfair – 'There is nothing, after all, in the marriage vows about "for better, for worse; for Parliament, for not"' – but it is simply a matter of facing up to reality. 'Obviously I would have liked to have spent more time with my husband, but I realised pretty early on that that was simply not going to be possible,' she says. 'As it worked out, I found fulfilment in my own interests as he found his in politics, and I think we came to value our time together very much more than we might have done if he'd had a more conventional job.'

The sense of movement and accomplishment in Norma's life was reinforced by the family's move to a more pukka address, Finings in Great Stukeley, which came with a mortgage attached that would not be paid off until 2050 (so John claims). The four-bedroomed mock-Tudor house had its drawbacks – it was just off the main road, it seemed a bit dark and depressing from the outside and it was a little too close to the US air base for comfort – but Norma grew to regard it as her sanctuary. Her whole life she had been moving around the country for the convenience of others but finally she felt that here she and her children were going to be allowed to settle. 'I think the day she walked into that house there was a sense of "this far and no further,"' says Margaret Marshall. 'It was the first place which she felt she could really call home.'

Certainly Norma had little time for the well-meaning friends who suggested that she had got her life 'upside down' and ought really to be down in London with her husband, who had lately been renting a flat in Brixton. Norma of all people knew quite how disruptive it could be for children constantly to be uprooted. 'When you get married, you make a conscious decision to have children and I think you should give them priority,' Norma has said, and then she added something which her mother, and perhaps her husband, would have found peculiarly painful to read: 'because you can't go back and retrieve that time together.'

Norma got into the routine of kissing John goodbye as he rushed for his train on Monday mornings and not seeing him again until the following weekend. It was inevitable, of course, with so much time spent apart, that the character of their relationship should change. There was no sudden parting of the ways: it was a slow, gradual process, manifest only after a few years when a number of their friends became aware that there were large areas of each of their lives that the other was entirely ignorant about. When John got home, often tired and bad-tempered, the last thing he wanted to talk about was what he had been doing at Westminster, and Norma, for that matter, never showed any interest anyway. She did not even trouble to go to the Commons to hear him make his maiden speech, something of a tradition among the wives of new MPs. Apart from the Atkins, who came to stay at Finings from time to time, she got to know few of his Westminster friends. For her, London had become another country.

Dulcie Atkins says that after a while MPs' wives who live apart from their husbands during the week tend to become so accustomed to the routine that they actually find it quite hard to readjust to having them around again for any length of time. 'To be perfectly honest, I often found the recess quite a strain,' she says. 'I suddenly had to come to terms with the fact that I couldn't just go out for as long as I wanted to because of course my husband was back at home.'

Nobody ever heard Norma complain about being separated from her husband for so much of the time, but then she was a Johnson woman. Both her mother and her grandmother had had to cope on their own, and it hadn't been their way to complain, or ever contemplate giving up; they just got on and made the best of things. And that Norma did. Neighbours like Mrs Winn, who had initially formed the impression that she was a rather delicate city lady, were soon marvelling at the way she hastily adapted to country life. She undertook most of the decorating of Finings herself, including the re-wiring, worked the rods on the septic tank on cold winter mornings and, infuriated by the way the rabbits from a nearby warren kept ploughing up her garden, she acquired a gun and proceeded to blast their brains out from her top-floor window. 'We were all very surprised when we started hearing the shots ringing out,' says Mrs Winn. 'The shy girl from London was turning out to be a lot tougher than we had imagined.'

Even the constituency functions were becoming slightly more palatable for Norma. She says that she actually enjoyed the dances. Her favourite partner was Sir David – he can dance me off my feet,' she said. John, alas, could only manage to 'shuffle' on the dance floor, she added dolefully.

Andrew Thomson left Huntingdon in 1982 to become the agent for Margaret Thatcher, the Prime Minister, at her Finchley constituency. Norma was desperately sorry to see him go, but she understood his reasons. Mrs Thatcher had taken on in Norma's eyes an almost god-like aura and she could see why he wouldn't be able to resist her call.

Thomson was succeeded as John's agent by Sheila Murphy, who continued to monitor Norma's progress. When she first met Norma, she says that she was struck by a woman who was still 'quiet and reserved, as distinct from shy, not in the least bit pushy. She didn't like having to perform publicly as the MP's wife, but if she absolutely had to do something, then she made up her mind and got on with it as best she could.' She feels that Norma's greatest contribution to life in the constituency was running a happy, well-organised home for John. As she says: 'Occasionally Westminster left him feeling very down and she was tremendous in building him up. You see, he worked so terribly hard. He would come up on a Friday late in the afternoon, and then he would do a surgery, then a function, and then at around 11.30 p.m. I would find myself in a car with him, worried to death that he might crash because he looked so drained.'

He would go home to Norma looking, as Miss Murphy says, 'very fed up and desperately tired'. She says with some under-statement that it was unlikely that he was especially good company on those evenings. Among his close friends John's temper was in fact legendary, despite his mild-mannered public image. Emily Blatch says that in private 'he can have quite a tongue on him'. That makes it all the more impressive that Miss Murphy says that she always used to find John 'transformed' when she came round on the Saturday to talk over constituency business. 'He always looked fine and ready for anything,' she says.

Norma continued to show no interest in politics – she still had no desire to see her husband speak in the Commons – but she took a very real interest in all the people she encountered. On one occasion Miss Murphy went to Finings on her birthday to drop in some papers for John. Only Norma remembered what day it was and on her arrival presented her with a present – an attractive sapphire-coated nail file. Miss Murphy could see that Norma was, however, becoming aware that what John was doing at Westminster was beginning to pose a threat to her ordered existence at Finings. After he was made the eastern area whip, with special responsibility for Northern Ireland, Special Branch detectives arrived at her home to improve security and to talk to her sternly about how she needed to be constantly vigilant. 'In her heart she hated it, but I think she realised it was essential,' recalls Miss Murphy. 'Obviously the idea that there might be people who would want to harm John frightened her, but she never spoke about it. She realised that it was just something else that she would have to come to terms with in her own way.'

It was during Miss Murphy's watch that Norma took a call from John while he was on a fact-finding mission with a dozen other MPs in the Middle East. He told her over a crackling line that a few days before he had been caught in crossfire between Palestinians and Israelis on the West Bank. When the *Cambridge Evening News* phoned up to talk about it, Norma's reaction was cool, almost detached: 'It was the first I'd heard about it. The line was bad and he didn't have much time. It came as a shock, but when I spoke to John he was obviously all right. There was no point panicking in retrospect.'

John's present agent, Peter Brown, succeeded Sheila Murphy in 1985 and found Norma doing the job 'about as effectively as anyone could'. She still wasn't making speeches, but Brown had no problem with that and wasn't in the business of making her do it if she didn't want to. 'I have seen some MPs' wives speaking and frankly it would make me cringe if I was married to any of them,' he says. 'Norma isn't a public speaker – and she accepts the fact. She is much, much happier talking to people, on a one-to-one basis. She is a bit like Princess Diana in that respect. Her constituency diary was and still is amazing. She is always opening something or doing something. She is a person who has always organised herself greatly: as a mother, a wife and a key player in the local constituency. She is tremendously conscientious. Once she agrees to do anything, she'll always make it, no matter what.'

There was some comment locally that although the Rentons had frequently entertained the Majors at the Moat House – and Major had once said publicly that David Renton meant more to him than anyone outside his family – the Majors had never once invited them back to their home. It was something that had hurt the old man rather more than he ever cared to admit. Part of it was that the Majors hated to permit political acquaintances or even friends across the threshold any more than was absolutely necessary, but it appeared that they were also consciously trying to live down the Rentons' memory. It certainly annoyed Norma that, socially and culturally, a lot of people still felt that she was her predecessor's inferior. Norma thought that she was still seen as 'a little person' who was worth talking to only on account of her husband's job. Even after Lady Renton's untimely death from cancer in 1986, Norma still felt the need to prove herself.

Norma's one great passion had always been opera. Her favourite performer was Joan Sutherland and it wasn't long before the idea of writing a biography of the diva began to take root. As a subject, it couldn't have been more worthy and she would have known very well that it would bring forth just the right reactions on the cocktail circuit. It would be something tangible that she could point to as evidence that she could do things on her own.

Almost as a hobby, to fill in the time while John was away, she had begun compiling a catalogue of Sutherland's performances since 1946, a fiddly, time-consuming task that nobody had undertaken before. She persuaded her friend Ian Cameron Black, a German speaker, and one of his colleagues, who spoke Italian, to write to the German and Italian opera houses for information. 'I told her that it would have been perfectly acceptable to have written to them in English, but she considered it a matter of common courtesy to write in the language of the recipient,' Cameron Black says. 'She was determined to do the job properly.'

As the task dragged on, Norma became aware that she had no hope of finding a publisher for a simple catalogue of performances. Her best hope was to present it as an appendix to a new biography of the diva. Norma did not consider that biographies should be written without their subjects' consent so she wrote to Sutherland to ask if she would mind very much if she wrote one on her. Sutherland, who vaguely remembered her from the days when she used to see her regularly outside stage doors in London, wrote back and said that she would be prepared to give the project her blessing, providing she could see it ahead of publication and make alterations as she deemed appropriate.

With Sutherland's seal of approval, the matter of finding a publisher became a mere formality. Norma set herself a strict regime to get the book written, setting her alarm for 5 a.m. to work on it so that it didn't interfere with getting the children off to school. During the school holidays, she headed off with Elizabeth in tow to the diva's palatial Swiss home. Sutherland, like Bronhill before her, liked Norma's diffident, understated manner. 'I knew she hadn't written any books before, but I had no doubt that she was up to the task,' she recalls. 'There was a kind of quiet confidence about her which dispelled my doubts.' A run of last-minute engagements meant that Sutherland was left with precious little time to speak to Norma so, instead, she took her to her study and left her contentedly copying from her scrapbooks of old newspaper cuttings. 'I remember that Norma said to me that she didn't want to disturb me any more than was absolutely necessary,' says Sutherland. 'For a biographer, I found that rather an endearing thing to say.'

Norma's research bore fruit: she wrote frankly about how gauche the young Joan had been in the early days of her career, there were entertaining accounts of her way of putting down colleagues who displeased her (to one she said: 'I thought *I* was supposed to be the *prima donna* here,') and, most striking of all, a frank account of how her elder sister Barbara committed suicide while she was still in her teens. Sutherland says: 'Norma never asked me about Barbara. I think that she would probably have liked to, but she just didn't seem able to bring herself to do it. What she wrote however was fair, presumably based on information she had gleaned from other sources.'

Writing the book was clearly a labour of love for Norma, but, as it always had to take its turn after her family and constituency responsibilities, it took more than ten years to write. She felt that the family regarded it as her little indulgence and occasionally it was a source of conflict in the household. So far from being supportive, Norma felt that they were often downright obstructive. Once, in exasperation at her husband's inability to recognise how important it was to her, she threw the heavy manuscript across the kitchen. Pages flew everywhere, some were never recovered. Chapter Five was found only when the washing machine had to be replaced, by which time she had alas rewritten it. From time to time, in moments of pique, she had a tendency to put the manuscript in the bin. On each occasion, John quietly fished it out and put it back on her desk. Although he evidently found her almost impossible to live with while she was writing it, he recognised that her quiet resentment if she had to abandon it would be far, far worse.

With the 1987 General Election looming, Norma had one last push to get the book finished. She sent it to Sutherland for her corrections and then to her publishers who appeared to have required some substantial rewriting. 'The final polishing up took longer than the rest of it,' says Sheila Murphy. The book which finally emerged was dedicated by Norma to 'my family' and she included a line in the acknowledgements about how grateful she was to John and the children for bearing with her, adding: 'I'm sure that they will not mind if they never see egg and chips or spaghetti bolognese again.'

Some of the reviewers' comments were good enough to quote on the back of the paperback edition: 'The best of the books about the diva' (*Opera* magazine); 'a major triumph' (*Daily Express*); 'Highly recommended' (*Scottish Opera News*), and, a little desperately, the verdict of the *Hunts Post* was there too: 'a well-written book, which is both interesting and enjoyable'. It failed, however, to make much of an impact on the cognoscenti. The veteran opera impresario Alan Sievewright considered it too cloying for his tastes and took exception to the way Norma appeared to be trying to ingratiate herself with her subject by running down her old rival, Maria Callas. Certainly some of the comments she made about her seem gratuitous: at one point, she noted that Callas 'was not exactly slight of physique', and, on another occasion, said that she agreed to be photographed with Sutherland 'with a graciousness that did not come easily to her'. Max Loppert, the chief critic of the *Financial Times*, agreed with Sievewright: 'very much the work of a fan as opposed to a serious student of opera,' he said. The *Guardian*'s opera correspondent Tom Sutcliffe found the book 'a self-satisfied and somewhat lazy portrait of the diva, confirming rather than challenging her view of herself'.

The one critic Norma had wanted to please most of all, Sutherland herself, professed herself delighted with it but then of course she had personally approved it before publication. She said that she preferred it to the two books that had previously been written about her. The first, by the Australian biographer Russell Braddon, was an authoritative but outdated work, and the second, by Quaintance Eaton, had, Sutherland felt, been marred by inaccuracies. 'The strength of Norma's book was its accessibility – it was written from the point of view of the ordinary fan,' she contends. 'Hers is the book that I referred to most frequently as I wrote my autobiography.'

Predictably, Norma resisted the blandishments of her publisher Alan Samson to go on any big promotional tour for the book. He had offered to hold a no-expenses-spared launch party in the Coliseum or the Royal Opera House, but Norma was having none of it. She insisted it should be held in the constituency – it had, after all, been for the constituents that she had written it. Samson noticed that at the party there were no London political types, except of course for John who seemed very proud indeed of his wife's achievement. It was the one time when Norma had no alternative but to make a short speech. John's agent Peter Brown says that the prospect of it had made her feel 'ill and drained', but, in the event, it was a perfectly respectable performance. She even got a laugh when she thanked her husband for retrieving the manuscript from the bin.

Norma told the *Cambridge Evening News* that the book had been like the arrival of a new baby: 'and it had been a long and

painful labour'. When somebody from the *Daily Express* asked
her why she didn't go to Westminster, her new-found sense of
independence came across loud and clear: 'I have got better
things to do than sit around in the Lobby waiting for John.'
Andrew Thomson, who was at the launch party, thought as he
watched her how far she had come since he first set eyes on her in
1976. 'Huntingdon has been good for her,' he thought to himself.

CHAPTER 4

The Glittering Prizes

O N THE WINDOWSILL at Finings, an old sepia picture of the man Norma was named after, her father Norman, takes pride of place. Sam Browne and badges of rank a-gleam, brilliantined hair, clipped moustache – he is frozen in a moment of time. On Norma's hand there is another reminder of him: his gold wedding ring which she always wears along with her own.

Having been deprived of a father herself during her formative years, Norma wanted above all things for John to be there for her own children. His swift rise through the ranks of Margaret Thatcher's government meant that that was not to be. History was to repeat itself.

John, like every Member of Parliament, has always liked to be seen as a good family man and knows the value of getting himself photographed in his garden with his wife and children, but this is of course just another of the many hypocrisies of Westminster life; there is nobody in national politics – certainly nobody with more than a passing interest in his career – who could possibly have the time to be a good family man. What newspaper readers so seldom realised when they saw pictures of John and Norma in the garden with their children was that it was a scene which happened maybe only once every few months, and even then they were not of course alone — there was always the photographer. In the pictures, John was always smiling his broad politician's smile; Norma, Elizabeth and James always seemed to look strained or sullen.

As John went further and further in his career, so his family inevitably became more distant — at best voices on the telephone or figures seen fleetingly over red boxes at weekends. From as long as the children could remember, Daddy always seemed to be at Westminster. It was Mummy to whom they turned if something was upsetting them or there was a problem at school. She was the one the teachers saw on parents' days and the big school events, seldom, if ever, John. The children would talk to him occasionally, but the conversations were almost always polite, diffident and sterile. One family friend remarks how strange it was that when he saw John with the children there never seemed to be any eye contact between them. There is a poignant picture of John and James taken at a football match which seems to prove his point: John is staring at James, who, obviously aware of it, is looking resolutely in front of him with a pained expression on his face.

That James and Elizabeth have grown up to become pleasant, well-adjusted young adults is — and everyone who knows the family says this — very much Norma's personal achievement. The people who criticised her for staying at home with them as they grew up never considered how things might have turned out if she had heeded their advice and gone to London and left the children to get on with it with a nanny or bundled them off to boarding-schools.

'Children with a father at Westminster face special pressures, special dangers and it is important for them to have somebody around,' says John's agent, Peter Brown. 'You look at Paul Channon and the loss of his daughter to drugs, you look at the Parkinsons and what they have been through, you look at Peter Shore, whose son is now dead. I don't blame any of them for any of this, but it all shows what *can* happen.'

The Majors' elder child, Elizabeth, is the most like John and accordingly the moodier of the two. Tall, coltish, with flowing light brown hair, she was one of the first girls to go to the nearby Kimbolton School after it went co-ed, and, though they weren't especially geared up for girls in the early days, she blazed a trail and became deputy head girl. She inherited her mother's taste for classical music and gave solo clarinet performances after winning her spurs with the Huntingdon Youth Orchestra.

The Rev. Ronald Lancaster, her divinity teacher at Kimbolton, says that, like her brother, Elizabeth was an average student, not an academic in the sense that there were any subjects which she lived for, but not someone whose progress ever caused him concern. She had a small coterie of very loyal friends at the school, but the person she was closest to was her brother. They would argue from time to time, but, underneath, she had a very protective attitude towards him. Her principal anxiety, Mr Lancaster says, was the media intrusion in her life as her father's career progressed. She made little secret of how much she hated the reporters who sometimes trailed her on her way to and from the school. Mr Lancaster got the impression, however, that Norma insulated her very effectively from the worst of the pressures associated with being John Major's daughter.

Elizabeth left school with A-levels in biology and social biology, but chose to help out at a local veterinary surgery instead of going on to university, which disappointed both John and Norma who had been hoping for Oxbridge. She has since moved on to work at the Animal Health Trust in Newmarket where she is regarded as a conscientious employee. It has been reported in the press and never officially denied that she works there as a trainee vet. She is actually only a trainee nurse at a salary of about £7,000 a year.

There is no serious boyfriend in Elizabeth's life at the moment. Animals, according to one friend, have been her life, and in the past they have been a cause of friction between her and her parents — she brooded for some months when they refused to buy her a horse, was horrified when she discovered that Norma was shooting the rabbits in the garden, and fought hard with John to get him to speak out against hunting in the Commons (conscious of the big rural vote in his constituency, he has, not surprisingly, been reluctant to acquiesce). John and Norma were also concerned when she joined a group of Baptists in the village. 'It got a bit heavy,' says Norma, but, much to her relief, Elizabeth later left the group.

On one occasion Elizabeth told a friend that she wished her father had 'a normal job'. A young lady of liberal views, she doesn't especially enjoy the company of the local Conservatives and one of her school friends speculates – no doubt mischievously – that she is independent-minded enough not to have been putting a cross in the obvious box at election times. Certainly she would have good reason to register a protest vote. She resents not just the press, but also, occasionally, the security arrangements at the house. Some of the Special Branch men she is inclined to treat like domestic servants. A reporter, who had come to Finings to interview Norma, says he was taken aback by the way Elizabeth walked into the house in a foul mood after being unable to get her car started on a cold morning and imperiously ordered a detective to 'go and sort it out'.

James is more like Norma. Peter Brown says that James has been the one who has been around when she has had problems and has helped her sort them out. Norma says that it is always James she turns to in a crisis, because he is more likely to respond willingly, rather than Elizabeth who might 'shrug a shoulder or pull a face'. Tall and athletic, with Norma's penetrating dark brown eyes, he has a laid-back approach to life and a ready if somewhat subversive sense of humour – he has been known to refer to a certain building in Smith Square as 'Gestapo headquarters'. He prefers what Norma calls 'heavy pop' to classical music and he enjoys parties at the local Conservative association, though he professes himself ignorant of politics.

At Kimbolton School, James's headmaster Roger Peel says that he is a popular boy, with his feet firmly on the ground. His great love is football, as a player and a dedicated supporter of Everton. After taking part in some trials for Aston Villa – which came about after John met the club's chairman Doug Ellis – he has now reluctantly accepted that his childhood dream of becoming a professional footballer is unrealistic. At sixteen, he passed all eight of his GCSE exams, is taking his A-levels, and has an open mind about university and a career, though there has been some talk of accountancy since he has a good head for figures. Norma says that she feels that it is important she leaves it to *him* to decide which career is best. 'I suppose, feeling so manoeuvred myself, I can't bear the thought of doing that to someone else.'

In no small measure, Norma has been helped over the years by her mother, Edith Johnson, who babysat for her while she was in London, and, when she moved to Huntingdon, took a flat in the nearby village of St Ives so that she could be called upon to help out when required. Norma's relationship with her is described by Emily Blatch as 'a very practical one'. A petite, bespectacled, white-haired lady, who sounds uncannily like Norma, she is fiercely proud of her son-in-law's achievements and keeps scrapbooks filled with newspaper cuttings charting his career. She latterly bought a house in Brighton, found she didn't like it, and moved back to London where she lives in a flat in Beckenham, a force in the local women's institutes – where she gives talks on Chequers – and a keen bridge player and maker of home-made wine. She still works three afternoons a week as a bookkeeper. She evokes contrasting opinions among her daughter's friends and in-laws. Norma keeps her away from the press as much as she can.

To Elizabeth, James and Mrs Johnson, Norma is undoubtedly a heroine, but no saint. When the pressures are mounting or she is pushing herself too hard, she invariably makes them aware of it. She bottles everything up, staggers on for as long as she can, and then explodes, often quite spectacularly: shouting, screaming and throwing things, followed by remorse and tears. It is a mélange of emotions which she describes as hormonal, and hints that she may be taking a course of hormone replacement therapy to counter it. The moods blow over quickly and the children, now used to them, pay little attention. 'Don't worry,' James nonchalantly told a visitor who turned up inopportunely. 'Mummy's just gone nuclear again.' His mother heard him and laughed.

Nothing has ever come easily to Norma. A reserved, very private person, it is the supreme irony that she should have found herself married to a man whose job so often requires her to be a public performer. She says that each step upwards that he has taken since he was selected for Huntingdon has terrified her, but she has never run away. For her, preserving the family has always been her overriding consideration, no matter what happens. As she knows very well, politics and most of the friends that you make in that world are transient: the family is what matters, it will still be there long, long after all the rest has gone.

As recently as the mid-eighties, Norma's life was a relatively straightforward affair. John was in the Whips' office and midweek would sometimes manage to get off early in the afternoon and have a quiet dinner at home with her and catch an early train back the next morning. At weekends, after he had attended to his constituency business, she would sit on the lavatory seat as he bathed and he would regale her with the latest Westminster gossip. She even got to accompany him to a dinner hosted by Margaret Thatcher at No. 10. She was very nervous about that, but when she took her seat she found herself a long way below the salt, which pleased her immensely because it meant that there were more people around her whom she would know. She still found it difficult to keep her eyes off Mrs Thatcher, to her, a shimmering, mythical figure at the head of the table.

John's junior post at the Department of Health and Social Security came not long afterwards, then Chief Secretary to the Treasury, each appointment, of course, bringing Norma in ever-closer proximity to the dreaded salt. People started to notice her husband; Norman Tebbit, to her great astonishment, even tipped him as a future leader of the party. John never spoke to her about his career. According to Olive Baddeley, he simply wasn't the type of man who could sit down in their front room and say: 'Darling, I think they're going to make me Foreign Secretary tomorrow.' Dulcie Atkins, the wife of the MP Robert Atkins, says that Norma was left to pick up things the way all Westminster wives tended to pick up things – by overhearing snippets of telephone conversations. By the summer of 1987, when the Majors and the Atkins went off on a canal boat holiday in the Midlands, Norma had a growing sense of unease about what lay ahead. She woke up one night covered in sweat and found that she had been clawing at a port-hole trying to get out. It was on that holiday that John, sitting at the bow with Robert, first discussed the possibility of him being a future contender for the premiership. At the time Norma and Dulcie were, symbolic-ally, sitting at the stern, neither of the men thinking to tell them about the hazardous course that they were plotting.

Norma's sense that the world was changing was reinforced not long afterwards when she heard of the death of Harry Simpson, a colleague of John's from his days on Lambeth Council, who had become a great friend of hers through their shared love of opera. He had died on his golden wedding anniversary and Norma immediately drove to Guildford to console his widow, Gladys. 'She arrived at 10 a.m. on the day he died and didn't leave until 7 p.m.,' remembers Mrs Simpson. 'We talked about the good times we'd had together. That day, for both of us, I think, life seemed better and simpler in Lambeth.'

As Norma was looking back, John was moving relentlessly forwards. On the day of Mrs Thatcher's cabinet reshuffle in the summer of 1989, Olive Baddeley telephoned Norma at Finings at 3 p.m. to ask if she had heard anything. 'No, nothing at all,' she replied. She phoned again at 5 p.m. and Norma sighed and said: 'There's nothing left now except for Transport.' Half an hour later John called and told her he had just been appointed Foreign Secretary in succession to Sir Geoffrey Howe. 'I don't believe it,' she said, gasping for breath. 'You're winding me up.' Moments later, as the news was still sinking in, Norma phoned Mrs Baddeley back and said: 'You'll never guess what's happened . . .' Mrs Baddeley says that Norma was devastated.

That evening Norma saw John standing proudly beside his gleaming official car with his bodyguard. Her face fell. John tried to cheer her up by joking that she should think positive and consider how lucky they were not to have to worry about parking any more. She couldn't laugh: she felt physically sick. What was going to be just another small step for John, was, all too obviously, going to be a giant leap for Norma.

Norma responded by plunging her roots deeper into the Cambridgeshire soil. The next morning she busied herself with her constituency chores. To the reporters who trailed her, caus- ing her considerable annoyance, she said peremptorily that for the time being she would be staying put. Her daughter happened to be about to take her A-levels and it was important that the routine was not disrupted. Finings would remain her base, but she would do what was required, within reason. She naturally wanted to do the right thing.

For a woman who clung so tenaciously to what was regular and ordinary, so much suddenly seemed irregular and extraordi- nary. Armed police officers moved in on Finings and took up residence in a caravan in the driveway. A fence was put up around the garden ('The one useful, practical thing I've ever got out of John's career,' she has told her friends. 'It means I don't have to worry about those wretched rabbits any more.') Super- ior, public-school-types from Whitehall telephoned her and wanted to know when she would be occupying her husband's two official residences: 1 Carlton Gardens, a magnificent town house in St James's, and Chevening, the 115-room country residence in Kent which was once the home of the Prince of Wales. She said that she had known about Carlton Gardens, but as for Chevening, she hadn't even been aware that that was part of the package. Not that it mattered really – she didn't see how she was going to fit either of them into her life in any case.

Of all the cabinet wives, the Foreign Secretary's has always had the most onerous role. It is a job which requires considerable social and diplomatic skills, acting as the hostess at big diplomatic functions. The prospect terrified Norma. She had always hated big, impersonal gatherings, and as for organising formal sit-down dinners, she admitted that she wouldn't know where to begin. The travelling which she imagined she would have to do as the wife of the Foreign Secretary seemed daunting, too – she hates flying, and, on the rare occasions that the family had holidayed abroad, she'd had to take travel sickness pills. Even going off in the car to Peterborough with Rosemary Juggins, she was prone to become 'a bit wobbly'. 'What you must understand is that Finings is where she feels she belongs,' says Mrs Juggins. 'The further away she is from it, the less secure she feels.'

Emily, now Baroness, Blatch says that after the appointment Norma had a feeling of being taken over by the government machine. 'She had something special at Huntingdon and she felt that it was being put under threat. She would ask me imploringly: "What on earth have we let ourselves in for?" To make matters worse, there is a frightfully snobby environment at the Foreign Office, which really wasn't her scene at all.' Barbara Wallis, John's constituency secretary, remembers that the men in Whitehall did not exactly go out of their way to make Norma feel welcome. 'They regarded her, at best, as a flaming nuisance, but then they regard all the ministers' wives as flaming nuisances for having the temerity to try to take up any of the ministers' time,' she says. 'They even issued her with a list of clothes – endless top-of-the-range ballgowns and tropical outfits – which they expected her to purchase as soon as possible in order to fulfil her duties. Of course they didn't offer to help with paying for them, and she was, frankly, a bit staggered by their attitude.'

There were some rather insulting suggestions too that Norma
might be well-advised to seek the services of a professional
makeup artist, to which she did not take too kindly, saying that
she was not prepared to be 'done over' by the image makers. She
told Barbara Wallis that she sensed from the outset that the civil
servants felt she was the sort of person who would eat her peas
off her knife, unless told otherwise.

In this kind of environment, feeling that everyone was watching her, just waiting for her to put a foot wrong, she inevitably
felt the strain. Robert Atkins thinks that she was not well, but
there was clearly more to it than that. Unbeknown to most of her
friends, she had just heard that her biography of Sutherland had
been remaindered. She had been asked by her publishers just a
few days before John's appointment if she would be interested in
writing a biography of the larger-than-life black opera star
Jessye Norman. She had told Dame Joan Sutherland that she had
been absolutely thrilled about it, had already made inquiries
about getting her authorisation, and couldn't wait to get started
– but of course John's appointment meant that there simply
wasn't going to be time, and, despondently, she had had to
withdraw. It prompted a columnist on the women's pages of the
Guardian to ask, perhaps not unreasonably, whether John might
have considered giving up *his* job to facilitate his wife's ambition. But such a question would of course never have occurred
to Norma. She quietly reconciled herself to the fact that her
husband's glittering prize was once again going to be her
sacrifice.

Dulcie Atkins says Norma was also 'worried sick' about how
John would fare with his new workload. Norma's concern for her
husband stemmed, it seemed, from a kind of inverted snobbery.
Not long before, she had been asked by a reporter, jokingly
almost, how she would feel if John were one day to become Prime
Minister. She replied, in deadly earnest: 'That sort of thing
doesn't happen to people like us.' To her, it seemed almost as if
her husband was a man who simply didn't know his place. Like

Icarus, he was making the mistake of flying too high and ran the risk of making a fool of himself by becoming unstuck.

To Norma, the way of life at the Foreign Office seemed entirely alien. Olive Baddeley says that she detested the rivalry among the wives at the diplomatic functions, refusing adamantly to take part in the ritual designer dress competitions and the behind-the-scenes bitching. The civil servants didn't help a great deal by allowing her to go into functions ill-prepared and badly briefed. They would give her typed lists of hopelessly old-fashioned 'dos' and 'don'ts' before each gathering – under headings such as To be Avoided (basically anything which could be construed as 'political', which tended to translate as relevant or interesting) and Suitable Subjects ('the ambassador's wife numbers needlework among her recreations'). With such limited material, the place setting next to the Foreign Secretary's wife was seen as something To Be Avoided by certain sections of the diplomatic community. It didn't help that Norma had such a poor memory. She could never remember people's names, even after they had been written down for her, and when she found herself in receiving lines, she says that she always spent too long talking to people and forgot the names of the ones who came afterwards.

Fleet Street too was putting pressure on Norma, wanting her to perform like her obliging predecessor Elspeth Howe (a lady who had been quite happy to be photographed curling up in a cardboard box for the night to draw attention to the plight of the homeless). With a great deal of reluctance, Norma eventually agreed to see a few writers from some of the more conspicuously Conservative newspapers. To all of them she put on the same front: she was an ordinary housewife muddling through in difficult circumstances. She pre-empted a lot of the criticisms that might have been made about her by a disarming honesty – 'I'm very happy with my lot, because I'm fulfilled by domesticity and I don't feel ashamed or guilty about that,' she told the woman from the *Daily Telegraph*. 'I have led a very cloistered life, but I don't feel any need to go out looking for adventure. I like the home and the family and the constituency, which is like an extended family. Beyond the constituency is no-man's land.' After making her acquaintance, even the acerbic *Daily Express* columnist Jean Rook – whom she had been desperately nervous about meeting – was moved to wonder: 'Am I naive in judging the Majors the straightest, homeliest, least devious political people I've met in years of interviewing MPs of all parties?'

Norma steeled herself to go with her husband on a trip to the United States, which, as it turned out, was rather less of an ordeal than she imagined. She met Barbara Bush for the first time, and, no doubt bringing out her famed maternal instincts, struck up an immediate friendship. Better still, she got to see a production of *Porgy and Bess* at the Metropolitan Opera during which John, as exhausted as ever, fell asleep beside her. Some things, at least, never changed.

But this was not a happy time for her; she made all of her friends -- everybody from Lord Rix to Peter Golds – aware of that. During the ninety-four days that John worked at the FO, she lost a stone in weight through worry. The appointment had taken John still further away from her and the children. The weekends – once sacred – were so often stolen from her as new crises kept blowing up in distant lands. The times she did get to have him on his own, his mind was often far away. She complained that he was missing all Elizabeth's clarinet classes and he hadn't seen James play football for ages. They might have seemed small things in the scheme of things, but to her they were the thin end of the wedge. They were starting to lose something which she had spent her whole life trying to build: the sense of being a family.

Even at Finings, Norma was unable to relax. During the summer she confided in Dulcie Atkins that she no longer felt happy about sitting on the sun-lounger in the back garden because she always had the feeling of being watched. She came to like some of the policemen stationed at the house very much – some of them she would occasionally lunch with in the local pub and even greet with a peck on the cheek when she returned after a long absence – but the truth was she never felt wholly at ease having them around. It wasn't them that worried her so much as what they represented – they were a constant reminder of the fact that John had made the whole family potential terrorist targets.

While John was Foreign Secretary, she made just a handful of visits to Chevening, so adored by the Howes. The first time she went to the grand old stately home was with a bucket and a mop in the back of her car because she imagined, correctly as it turned out, that it could probably do with a good clean, having been left unoccupied for so long. One weekend in October she went to Carlton Gardens, where, once again, she spent almost the whole time cleaning – this time scrubbing the white plastic headboards. She had had it in mind to get it into a reasonably fit state so that she could spend the occasional weekday night there with John (who, to his eternal shame, had already been living contentedly with the offending headboards for some months).

As it turned out, Norma had laboured in vain. The following Monday, John was appointed Chancellor of the Exchequer after Nigel Lawson's resignation. Judy Hurd wasted no time moving into Carlton Gardens with Douglas, and, funnily enough, one of her first acts upon entering the building was to order that all the headboards be put out for the binmen. 'They were 1960s relics,' she laughs. 'The white plastic was never going to look clean, however hard you scrubbed them.' The headboards were fortunately not mentioned when Norma phoned up to wish Mrs Hurd well as her successor. There was an almost palpable sense of relief in her voice that her own stint was over. 'I am sure that Norma would have liked it once she had got into it,' says Mrs Hurd. 'I think it was just the thought, "Help, can I do this?" The fact is you don't *have* to do anything as the Foreign Secretary's wife. Of course a whole crowd of people want to get to know you, and ask you to do things. But I suppose you could quite happily say: "I can't do it all. I've got a career and other commitments and I can't fit all this into my life."'

From the outset Norma felt far happier about the idea of being the wife of the Chancellor. It was a much more congenial role: all that seemed to be required of her was to stand beside her husband on the steps of No. 11 for the time-honoured budget day photo-calls. (Her blue Jacques Vert suit would be just the thing, she thought.) Of course it was horses for courses – the energetic Edna Healey, when she was the Chancellor's wife, hated every minute of it because there was so little for her to do. Norma loved it precisely for that reason.

The Chancellor's personal safety is curiously not deemed as important as the Foreign Secretary's and, accordingly, the police moved their caravan out of the driveway at Finings, and, for Norma, life seemed to be finally getting back to normal. The *Cambridge Evening News*, by now accustomed to chronicling the promotions of their local MP, routinely telephoned Norma to ask whether she would be following Thérèse Lawson's example and moving her family to No. 11, and whether she would have any use for Dorneywood, the Chancellor's official residence. She gave the routine reply that she would be staying put. James was at Kimbolton, Elizabeth had her job and she had her commitments in the constituency: it was of course out of the question.

Perhaps it was just as well that Norma did not go to London. The sight of the urbane Mrs Hurd settling down with such aplomb at Carlton Gardens with her young children would have been singularly disconcerting for her. Mrs Hurd had spent the previous six years living in government houses, and, therefore, had no trouble making herself and her family at home at her new residence. An unaffected, decent woman, she was embarrassed to find that just about everything she said and did seemed to draw attention to her predecessor's apparent intransigence. 'I regard having a family-sized house within easy reach of White-hall and the House of Commons as a real bonus,' she says. 'It has meant that the children and I have not been separated from Douglas's life. I always aim to make a government house feel like home. This one is now full of books and toys and musical instruments and parts of our life. I would hate it any other way.'

The men at the FO did not consider it necessary to issue Mrs Hurd with a clothes list, and she was able to put her foot down effectively when they tried giving her their 'dos' and 'don'ts'. 'When a new Minister is appointed, they soon get to know what sort of animal his wife is,' Mrs Hurd points out. 'If we are entertaining a foreign minister and his wife, I like to have a serious brief. There seemed to be a feeling that a wife's brief had to be very banal, sort of women's talk, which simply isn't relevant any more. Women want to talk about what everybody else is talking about. They don't want to talk about their clothes and their hair or whether it is a good idea to go to Chanel for clothes. That was all based on the days when women were expected to withdraw at the end of dinner. What I like if I am having dinner with, say, the Turkish Foreign Minister, is a brief saying what's happening in Turkey and what the problems are in that country.'

The confident Mrs Hurd found no oneupmanship among the wives of the visiting statesmen – 'I *enjoy* my colleagues,' she says – and, as for the travelling, she reveals that she loves it. 'I like the new interests that the FO has given me, so I am very happy to fit in as much as I can. It is a privilege and an education.'

As the Chancellor's wife, Norma soon found that although she had more time to herself, she could spend precious little of it with John, whose workload was heavier than it had ever been before. At a dinner in the City, a businessman leant over to her and said: 'I'd very much like a quiet word with your husband.' Norma replied with some feeling: 'So would I.' Even when John came home at weekends, he would haul his red boxes on to their double bed at 6.30 a.m., waking Norma up. 'The whole bed shakes,' she complained in an interview. 'It's bloody selfish really. I'd love to pick one up and shake it all over the place.'

She still tried to do her bit, however. Olive Baddeley says that Norma once baked some biscuits for the guests to eat at a function at No. 11 when John was handing out some long-service awards. She also went to see John deliver his Budget statement in the Commons, but, Mrs Baddeley says, she left early because she was meeting a friend for tea.

A year after John became Chancellor, he had to make an enforced stay at Finings to recover from an operation on a peculiarly painful wisdom tooth. It coincided with a moment of high drama within the Tory party: Sir Geoffrey Howe's bravura resignation as Deputy Prime Minister followed by the plots and rumours of plots. Norma was made as aware as anyone of the rumblings of discontent as she found herself continually answering phone calls from John's parliamentary colleagues who were eager to know if he would be standing in any leadership contest. There had even been a suggestion from Norman Lamont that it might have been politically expedient for John to have postponed his operation. Norma had reacted with scorn to that: she would not have her husband thought so desperate to push his way into No. 10 that he would prolong his agony. As John recovered, she said to all but his closest friends that he wasn't well enough to come to the phone.

The idea of a plot against Mrs Thatcher struck Norma as pretty unsavoury and she made little secret of the fact that she didn't like the idea of her husband becoming embroiled in it. She had idolised the woman, and, her being a Conservative running a poor second to her being a member of the human race, she had nothing but contempt for the vultures who were already hovering overhead. As hard as she tried, however, she could not keep John away from London for long. Twelve days after Sir Geoffrey's speech, Michael Heseltine, the former defence secretary, announced his intention to stand against Mrs Thatcher for the party leadership. On 22 November, Mrs Thatcher, with tears in her eyes, told the cabinet that she would be stepping down. Norma, watching the drama unfold on her television set at Finings, felt so sorry for her that she wanted to give her a big hug. It was a very typical reaction. Had she a more political nature, she would immediately have wondered whether John was also going to stand for the leadership. As it happened, that was exactly what he did do, before the day was out, along with Douglas Hurd, the Foreign Secretary.

It did not of course go unnoticed in Fleet Street that all the candidates in the leadership contest were married. The thought of a Tory Prime Minister's wife — a life-form extinct in Britain since Lady Home more than quarter of a century before — stirred the imaginations of the news editors. All of them wanted long analyses of the respective merits of the three wives. To many observers, it seemed another unwelcome Americanisation of the political system; a particularly virulent form of 'First Lady Syndrome' had reached Britain's shores. It was probably more appropriate to blame *Hello!* magazine and the insatiable appetite that it had helped to create for new personalities, no matter who they were or what relevance they had. Loyd Grossman wrote a flippant piece in the *Daily Express* in which he observed that, from the point of view of the electorate, the candidates' wives were a good thing: 'Think of it as a bargain — elect one, get one free: the great first lady offer. With every Michael, a free Anne; with every Douglas, a free Judy; with every John, a free Norma.'

Within hours of the announcement of John's candidacy, reporters started ringing, asking for interviews. Almost all of them began with the same line: 'We've already spoken to Mrs Hurd and Mrs Heseltine and we wondered if we could talk to you, too.' There was an implied threat in that — 'If you don't talk to us, you'll look as if you're the only one who isn't prepared to play the game' — to which Norma did not take kindly, and, besides, the idea of being thrown into the ring with the other two wives to be judged like prize poodles didn't appeal to her in the slightest. She didn't see why she should be *expected* to perform: for all they knew, she could have been an agoraphobic. She also happened to think that it was a waste of time because John wasn't going to win anyway. When Robert Atkins came on the phone she asked, as if inquiring of the prospects of a three-legged gelding in the Grand National: 'John doesn't *really* have a chance, does he?'

Norma resolved to stay at Finings for the duration of the campaign. She would talk to the local paper and one or two others from the nationals, but they would have to come to her, and they would have to be fitted in around her constituency engagements. That would be the extent of her personal campaigning. To those she saw, she endeavoured to make the right noises. When the man from the *Cambridge Evening News* asked her if she thought her husband was going to win, she replied: 'You do not go into these things without being positive about them,' which didn't quite sound the same as 'Yes'.

The two women whom she was being pitted against, Judy Hurd and Anne Heseltine, were of course in London where the action was, and performing for the national media with a considerably greater degree of enthusiasm. Consummate Westminster wives both of them, they had reasoned that if newspapers were prepared to give them space to put the case for their respective husbands, it would be less than supportive of them not to play along. Mrs Heseltine was even prepared to talk to the *Guardian* and the *Daily Mirror*, neither of them newspapers on many Tory MPs' reading lists. In their innumerable interviews, the two wives did their best to appear magnanimous about Norma, the conspicuously absent wife, but subtly drew attention to her main drawbacks as a potential Prime Minister's wife. 'She is very special, very quiet,' said Mrs Hurd. 'She is shy – but there's no reason why that should be a problem,' remarked Mrs Heseltine.

It is an understatement to say that Mrs Heseltine and Mrs Hurd were both thinking rather more positively than Norma. Asked about how she felt about the prospect of her husband becoming the Prime Minister, Mrs Hurd said: 'It will not be easy. I will have to divide myself up, but I think I could do that. I know I could.' Mrs Heseltine, for her part, sounded like a contestant for

November 1990: Norma Major standing beside her husband after his surprise victory in the leadership contest. Friends said that she was in 'a state of shock'. (*Times* Newspapers Corporation)

The old Post Office in All Stretton,
where Norma began her life.

Norma on the steps of
St Matthew's Church, Brixton,
after her marriage
to John.

A lucky escape? Bette Grainger,
the young woman who so nearly
became Mrs John Major.

May 1979: John and Norma
acknowledge well-wishers after
John's election as Huntingdonshire's
MP. The role of constituency wife
was to be a formidable challenge
for Norma.

LEFT: June Bronhill with Keith Michell
in *Robert and Elizabeth*, in London in
1964. Some of the dresses for the
production were made by Norma.

Norma doing her bit for charity
with her close friend, Emily Blatch.
(*Cambridge Evening News [C.E.N.]*)

A family photo-call for John and Norma with Elizabeth who looks, as ever, none too enthusiastic about being used as a human prop. (*C.E.N.*)

The strain tells on Norma's face at a public function three days after John became Chancellor. 'I suppose it's good news,' she said of the appointment.
(Press Association [P.A.])

Norma sits out the Tory Party leadership campaign at home at Finings. (*C.E.N.*)

LEFT: Norma during one of just a small handful of interviews she gave during the leadership campaign. (*C.E.N.*)

RIGHT: A weary-looking Norma in full retreat from No. 10. (*P.A.*)

Hours after the IRA's mortar-bomb attack on Downing Street, Norma is out in the constituency starting a Pancake Day race. (*C.E.N.*)

Downing Street's new residents as seen by *Spitting Image*. Fluck and Law celebrate Norma's gift to John of a satellite TV dish, so that he could watch his cricket. (Central TV)

Norma indulging in one of her favourite pastimes – bellringing – for television's *Help Squad*. (T.V.S.)

First among equals? Norma plays host to the other world leaders' wives at the G7 summit, her friend Barbara Bush at her side. (P.A.)

John stops Norma from
making an untimely escape
at the 1992 Tory Party
conference in Brighton!
(P.A.)

Still jetlagged after their world
tour, Norma insisted John
accompany her to look at
bathroom fittings. (*C.E.N.*)

The only known picture of the whole family together outside the door of No. 10 after the General Election result – John, Norma, Elizabeth and James (P.A.)

Norma puts wheelchair-bound Heather Strudwick and her sister
Patricia Crittenden at their ease at a Downing Street reception (P.A.)

A horrified Norma sees her daughter Elizabeth fall from her mount at the
Huntingdon Steeplechases. (*Today*/Rex Features)

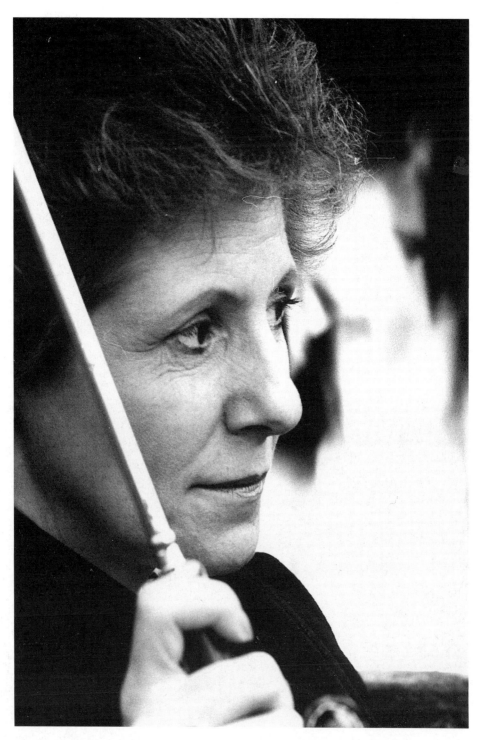

Another day, another public engagement for Norma Major,
the reluctant celebrity. (*C.E.N.*)

Miss World — 'It's a chance to meet lots of people' — but nobody doubted her determination to see her husband win. Norma's response to the question, by contrast, sounded weary, almost truculent: 'I am sure it is very naive of me, but, having been through the last eighteen months, which has been a difficult struggle, I would like to think we can carry on as we are.'

Mrs Heseltine and Mrs Hurd used their interviews to counter systematically the accusations that were being made about their respective husbands and to play up their good points. The former had noticeably more accusations to deal with than the latter. There was the charge that her man was power-hungry ('People came to *him* and asked *him* to stand'); out of control ('He never did swing that mace. Somebody jogged him'); humourless ('With children like ours, he's had to take jokes against himself'); a dandy ('It takes a real effort to make him buy a suit'); had a silly hairstyle ('It's very difficult hair. You can't part hair like that because he has a double crown and it just stands up in spikes!'); even that he had strangled the family Alsatian ('The dog got a thorn in its paw which my husband inadvertently pressed and the dog went for him. He got the dog by the collar and twisted it. The dog coughed and then stopped and later had to be put down').

Mrs Heseltine worked just as hard when it came to posing for the photographers and she knew precisely what she wanted from them: 'I *hate* looking over my shoulder, it looks too antagonistic,' she told one. 'And I'm a bit wary of these shoulder-pads. They make one look a bit deformed.' It was only on the issues that she disappointed. Asked about her thoughts on feminism, childcare and abortion, she murmured: 'They've sort of resolved themselves, haven't they?' She said something about her fears for elderly people living alone, and then added weakly: 'But I don't want to misrepresent myself as a social campaigner.'

Of the three wives, Mrs Heseltine had easily the most impressive CV. She listed on it her honours degree in modern languages, courses in art history, a partnership in a gallery dealing in nineteenth-century French art, membership of the arts advisory group to the South Bank and of the Furniture and History Society as well as what she called 'the obvious activities involved in being an MP's and subsequently cabinet minister's wife'. But there was an unmistakably regal air about the woman which a lot of people found off-putting. She would think nothing of spending around £3,000 a season at Yves Saint-Laurent's Rive Gauche shop, a habit that was politically rather awkward in a recession. So imperious was she that, according to legend, she once looked blankly at Margaret Thatcher when she told her she had been shopping at Safeway. 'And what,' Mrs Heseltine reportedly asked her, 'is *Safeway*?'

Norma's friends are inclined to draw comparisons between her and Anne Heseltine, saying disparagingly that she is 'the typical politician's wife', and hinting that whereas Norma might be homely and a bit shy, her rival was cold and downright pushy, which was eminently less palatable. One even calls her 'the bitch in boots', a reference to a revue she once appeared in for the Bicester Hunt, dressed in a white top hat and tails and wielding a whip. That Mrs Heseltine possessed a stronger political instinct than Norma seemed beyond doubt. When she heard the news of Geoffrey Howe's resignation on her car radio, she admits that she nearly skidded off the road. Unlike Norma, she saw immediately what the news could have meant for her husband and herself. If Norma sometimes resembled Trollope's character the Duchess of St Bungay, a lady happy to leave the vulgar business of politics to her husband, then Mrs Heseltine would have to be Lady Glencora Palliser, a woman who devoted herself entirely to her husband's career and determined to make him the most powerful Prime Minister who ever lived.

It is harder to suggest which character from Trollope Mrs Hurd might resemble. On the surface, her homely manner and wistful remarks gave the impression that she was another reluctant Westminster widow, a natural soulmate of Norma, but, having spent some years working in the Commons as her husband's secretary, she had developed a political instinct almost as sharp as Mrs Heseltine's, but perhaps better concealed. When she drove up to her home and saw a crowd of media people outside on the day that her husband declared his candidacy for the leadership, she shrewdly decided to leave some dirty sheets she had in the back of the car where they were because she realised that to be photographed bundling them into the house would not project the right image as a prospective first lady.

Mrs Hurd also used her press interviews to great effect. Conscious that her husband was seen to have come from a privileged, patrician background, she was keen to portray him as a man of the people. She referred to him as 'Doug', said that she didn't see him as being in the least bit aloof, and affected shock on one occasion when a reporter suggested to her that she might wish to send a maid out to Fortnum's to help her through the campaign week. 'Oh no, it's a case of Sainsbury's . . . or maybe Waitrose,' she said. To inject a little human interest, she spoke about her first date with Doug ('He put his hand on mine. I pulled it away') and told an endearing story about how she had warned her five-year-old son Philip that his father might soon be the Prime Minister. The boy had replied: 'Does that mean he won't have time to play chess with me any more?'

So far from point scoring, Norma, by contrast, dwelt on matters that her rivals had thought it best to stay clear of – her sadness about the manner of Mrs Thatcher's departure (at a point in history when 'Thatcherite' was a dirty word, she admitted: 'I am one of her biggest fans'), her reluctance to move to No. 10, her determination to keep the children out of the limelight, and how at all costs she wanted to preserve her life in Huntingdon. The only time she actually spoke up for her husband was when she dismissed a suggestion that he was too young and inexperienced for the job, saying that he was roughly the same age as the labour leader Neil Kinnock, but by comparison had experience of top government jobs. (An odd point to make.

seeing that it wasn't of course Kinnock that John was competing with for the Tory Party leadership.)

As a gesture of solidarity during the campaign, Norma telephoned Mrs Hurd. 'The message was that we were all going through it together and that she, like me, was looking forward to it being over,' says Mrs Hurd. 'It helped to ease the situation a bit.'

Mrs Hurd says that she was surprised by the degree of attention the media were paying to her as one of the candidates' wives. 'There was a feeling of being under siege. Every time I went out of the door with the children we were photographed. It all seemed rather overblown. Journalists kept asking for interviews, and one felt that if one didn't see them they would just dredge up all the old stuff from their files. And, most of all, one wanted to try to do something to help — even though when one had done it, one wasn't sure if it helped or hindered. The truth is I don't think it made an iota of difference.'

After an inconclusive first ballot, Mrs Heseltine stood shoulder to padded shoulder with her husband on the steps of their Belgravia home on the day of the second ballot. She gazed adoringly up at him with both fingers crossed and a broad smile on her face. She had even had a new hairstyle for the occasion — her 'prime ministerial wave'. The photographers adored it.

Mrs Hurd, aware that her husband had become the outsider in the race, elected to keep in the background that morning. People who saw her said that she was perfectly cheerful, but reconciled to her husband losing.

Norma went about her chores with what one of her friends called 'a strangely unperturbed air'. It had been her belief that Michael Heseltine was going to win: to her mind, people like that tended to become prime minister. When the results finally came through, there was no outright winner, but, rather than let it go through to a third ballot, Douglas Hurd and Michael Heseltine both announced their support for John, in the interests of party unity. Mrs Heseltine stood despondently beside her husband as he conceded defeat. The prime ministerial wave suddenly looked very limp.

Mrs Heseltine's friends say that she was deeply distressed by what happened. Even now she finds it too painful to talk about. 'My husband and I have made a point of refusing all interviews on the subject as it is now very much in the past,' she says. 'We feel that enough has been said on the subject.' That's a basic rule in politics: don't talk about your defeats unless you have to.

Although she had thrown herself into the campaign with gusto, Mrs Hurd was not especially put out by what had happened. With it all behind her, she admits: 'I should think it would have been hell to have been the Prime Minister's wife. There is now no chance of that happening. I think that is one we can safely put behind us.' She even felt at liberty to tell another story about her son Philip, a very different story to the one that she had told during the campaign. 'On the day before the ballot for the leadership, I told him that Daddy *wasn't* going to win as he walked up the stairs one night before going to bed. He was rather upset; he thought Daddy won everything. As if to make it up to me, he said: "Don't worry, Mummy, I think I might be Prime Minister one day."'

As the Foreign Secretary's wife, Mrs Hurd feels that she has quite enough to contend with. She admits that she worries about whether it is possible to fulfil the role and be a good mother to her two children, who are both under ten. She says that she finds it difficult to divide her family's life between three homes – Chevening, Carlton Gardens and their home in Oxfordshire – and says it takes a monumental degree of organisation even to ensure that there is a clean shirt waiting in each of them for Douglas. 'I do look forward to the day when I will be able to go back to looking after my chickens in Oxfordshire,' she confesses.

Of Norma, she says: 'I like and respect her. She is interesting and intelligent and she has dignity. I think that she is good at deciding what she wants to do with her life. She hasn't tried to do everything. She has been directional and disciplined. She concentrated on her children when they needed her and I think that was absolutely right.'

The Duchess of St Bungay had triumphed over Lady Glencora Palliser. It is a strange thing, but the wives who have most wanted to play the part of the Prime Minister's wife over the years have almost always been disappointed. Ironically, it has been the ones who have most shrunk from it who have invariably been forced to play it.

CHAPTER 5

The Woman in Blue

W HEN THE NEWS broke at 6.36 p.m. on 27 November 1990 that John Major had won the leadership contest and was to succeed Margaret Thatcher as Prime Minister, Norma's reaction was one of shock. Not shock as in surprise, but clinical shock, the sort people get after hearing of the death of a close relative or being involved in a serious accident. But then the woman had just been hit hard by something very big that had come at her at considerable speed. 'I didn't regard it as a particularly joyous occasion,' Norma says, with some understatement. 'I took several months really to sort it out. Things were happening to me that I wasn't prepared for.'

Within ten minutes of the announcement, officers from the Metropolitan Police and the local force moved in on Finings along with what seemed like an army of workmen and engineers. There was an almighty commotion. Alarms, surveillance equipment and a hotline to No. 10 were hurriedly installed. In the garden, work began on an outhouse to accommodate members of the Prime Minister's permanent security unit. The family were told to keep away from the windows until the bullet-proof glass was installed. Two men wearing balaclavas and armed with sub-machine-guns menacingly took up positions in the driveway.

At the gates to the house, newspapermen and television crews were massing. Every arrival and departure, even James's, was accompanied by barrages of flashlights and shouted questions. On the day that her husband had become the most powerful man in Britain, Norma found herself powerless to defend even her own home.

In the aftermath, Norma told well-wishers that it just didn't seem real. When they referred to the Prime Minister, she kept thinking that they were talking about Mrs Thatcher. All of them had expected her to be deliriously happy, but were struck by the sombre note in her voice. Peter Golds felt that she had seemed more impressed when she discovered that John was a councillor. 'She could cope with Lambeth Council – that was success on a manageable scale for her, but this was simply too much.' After talking to her, Maggie Scott felt that it had 'all happened too quickly. She could have handled John becoming Prime Minister in a few years' time, but not then, not that soon.' Norma's remark to Ian Cameron Black contained more than a hint of bitterness: 'Well,' she said, 'John has got what he wants, hasn't he?'

To Sue Winn, Norma said: 'I don't think I'd ever realised what John's ambitions really were. He was so thrilled to be the Chancellor. I don't think I had ever looked beyond that.' She told Olive Baddeley that she imagined she would only have to spend a few days in London and then she would be able to get back to normal. Pat Dessoy, Norma's sister-in-law, says: 'I was left wondering whether she had realised now that John was Prime Minister to what extent it was going to involve her as well.'

'Norma just *hates* it when unexpected things happen,' says Nesta Wyn Ellis, one of John Major's biographers. 'She told me once that she only really liked watching films she had seen before because she could be sure that she would like them.'

Norma's first thoughts as ever were for the children. They were to be protected at all costs. She was adamant that they were not to be dragged into the burgeoning media circus down in London and forbade them both from attending John's victory party. She told Elizabeth that she could come down to London the following day but she was to stay at Finings that night. She allowed James to go out to celebrate at the local Conservative Association. It was going to be difficult, she knew, but they were both to try to keep away from the reporters.

When Norma arrived at the hastily-arranged victory party in Downing Street, she walked up to her husband and stood beside him. He put his arm around her, whispered something in her ear, smiled at her, and was then swept away from her in the throng. She was left standing alone in a corner of the room, in silence, looking at the ground. Amid all the ribaldry and extravagant glad handing, she took on the air of the spectre at the feast. Robert Atkins says that she plainly hadn't come to terms with the news and most of the people there thought it best to let her be. The feeling was that she simply needed time.

David Mellor, another guest, says that she seemed 'numbed'. He believes that after Mrs Thatcher's resignation, the pace of events had been such that John hadn't had a chance to sit down with Norma and talk through what it would mean to her if he became Prime Minister. Olive Baddeley feels that, at the back of his mind, John would have known that it would be difficult for Norma if he won, but she doubts, frankly, if he had realised quite how difficult.

Norma quietly slipped out of the party at one point to take a call. Baroness Blatch, concerned about her, went to look for her and found her in the kitchen, holding the telephone, telling somebody that she understood, that she was terribly sorry, that she was not to cry. It turned out to be her old friend, Gladys Simpson. A journalist had phoned trying to pick up an anecdote or two on John, and had inadvertently asked to speak to her husband Harry, who had died some years ago. Mrs Simpson knew that it was silly, but it had made her cry and she had just wanted to talk to someone. Norma told her that she understood.

Already that day a frail, elderly friend of hers in Bourn had been driven to distraction by reporters calling at her home. At

Finings, her mother, with no experience of dealing with the press, was having to field calls from every newspaper in the land. In the suburbs, Pat Dessoy, her sister-in-law, had been visited by a stranger with an Irish accent – with no ulterior motive, as it turned out, but it had still terrified her. Her brother-in-law Terry Major-Ball says that he had been 'traumatised' when he had looked out of his bedroom window and seen newspapermen gathering outside. 'At least when you are Prime Minister you know what needs to be done – it isn't so clear when you are the Prime Minister's brother, sister, wife or even his friend,' he points out. 'Unfortunately there aren't any books which you can get at the local library to tell you what to do.' James, at the party in Huntingdon, hadn't been able to get out of giving his first newspaper interview. There was a quiet dignity about what he told the reporter: 'I am very excited and extremely pleased. I don't know much about his life in politics, but, as far as I am concerned, he's the best Dad I could have. But I suppose it will mean that I will see even less of him now.'

Norma hated the way the lives of so many other people were being disrupted by her husband's achievement. But none of their lives was being disrupted quite as much as her own. All of a sudden, she was expected to sleep in the surprisingly cramped, inhospitable private quarters above No. 10 and be at the beck and call of the Prime Minister's staff. They were very courteous, his staff, very well-spoken, matchless when it came to observing the social graces, but she had the unnerving feeling that they weren't asking her to do things. They were *ordering* her.

When they wanted her to stand beside her husband for his press conference outside No. 10, they told her where to stand, where to look, and not to say anything. Still numbed, still dazed, she stood there, blinking, trembling, and a little hunched up like a small girl expecting to be smacked. She could just make out some of the faces of the reporters under the raw, white glare of the TV arc lights. They were just staring, not smiling, quite expressionless, pushing and shoving to get a better view, yelling questions at John, writing them down, recording them.

At one point she let out a giggle as her husband made his speech. It was only nerves – he had not said anything funny – but it did not go unnoticed. Nothing went unnoticed. Some of the reporters' questions were directed at her. 'Mrs Major, how do you feel?' one of them shouted. She looked back, confused, gesturing, mouthing, but the words did not come; the helpless, anguished expression on her face horribly redolent of Edvard Munch's *The Scream*.

Those who had known Norma all her life were transfixed by the woman they saw on their television sets. 'I was struck by the way that she hadn't changed at all,' says Catherine Shadbolt (*née* Evans), who had known Norma from her days in All Stretton. 'She looked and acted just as she had when she last came to stay with us in her early teens.' Anne Smart, Norma's headmistress from Peckham School for Girls, had the same feeling that she was watching someone from her past who had been mysteriously frozen in time: 'It was as if she was taking morning assembly thirty years ago. It was quite uncanny.'

Pauline Hallanzy (*née* Glover), her old classmate from the school, says: 'At first I couldn't believe it was her. She seemed familiar but I just couldn't equate the woman standing outside No. 10 with the little Norma that I had known. It seemed inconceivable.' And no, Mrs Hallanzy adds that she didn't find it reassuring to think that somebody whom she had grown up with could make it on to the world stage. 'I'd rather not have had anything to do with her,' she insists. 'That way perhaps I might have had some respect.' Richard Finny, June Bronhill's former husband, says that he just laughed. 'There she was again – standing beside that funny little man I had teased all those years ago, and, you know, neither of them had changed a bit.'

The one person who couldn't bear to see her first big appearance on national television was Norma herself. The gauche

provincial whom she saw standing beside John seemed to con-
firm her worst fears about herself. It was a time when she
desperately needed somebody like Andrew Thomson around to
build her up, but instead all she got was unrelenting, wounding
criticism. 'She looked like a rabbit caught in headlamps,' was
how one newspaper reported her performance at her first press
conference. 'An exercise in how *not* to behave when you have just
become the First Lady,' sneered another.

Norma was consoled over the telephone by her mother. Mrs
Johnson tried to make her feel better by saying that she wasn't
the one who should feel hurt – if they were attacking anybody,
they were attacking *her*, because they were implying that she
hadn't brought her up properly. The conversation then turned to
practical matters. Mrs Johnson said that she was aware that
Norma would be running short of clothes in London, so she
would pack some new outfits into an old John Lewis bag and ask
Olive Baddeley, who was coming to London to do some interviews, to bring them with her.

Unfortunately Mrs Baddeley did not make it to London in time
for Norma's visit to Buckingham Palace with John to receive the
historic seals of office from the Queen. So as they were getting
ready to go, she had a dilemma: dare she wear the same blue
Jacques Vert suit which she had worn on the night of her
husband's victory? She asked John about it, who said, distract-
edly, that he always thought she looked nice in it, and if she felt
comfortable in it, then fine, she should wear it.

At the Palace, in her comfortable old blue suit, Norma was led
into the Equerry and Waiting Room where she was looked after
by the Duchess of Grafton while John had his audience with the
Queen. The Duchess, the Mistress of the Robes to Her Majesty
the Queen, warmed to Norma immediately. 'She had this marvellous sense of wonder at being in Buckingham Palace,' she
recalls. 'I suppose one gets so used to people being blasé, but here
was somebody for whom it all really meant something.' The
Duchess tried not to make the occasion any more onerous for her

guest than necessary and kept the conversation to homely matters such as her children, and, topically, the perennial problem all ladies face in public life: knowing what to wear.

As Norma was telling the Duchess how very difficult it was to match the outfit to the occasion, the fashion writers were sitting down at their word processors to pass judgement on the blue suit that they had seen her wearing on her way to the Palace (*and* on Budget day a few months before, but fortunately that slipped their minds). One said it had looked pretty hideous the first time around, and, seeing it again so soon, she saw no reason to revise her opinion. Even the executives at Jacques Vert were rumoured to be dismayed to be associated publicly with such a dowdy woman.

Fleet Street, lost for words at Norma Major's behaviour, turned to the psychologists for explanations. One was quoted in the *Daily Mirror* as saying: 'By wearing that shapeless suit once again, she was letting people know "I'd really rather not be here." It seems that she will always want to be Mrs Ordinary. Dressed like that, she's the kind of woman you would walk straight past in the street – and that's just what she wants you to do.' Dr Robert Cohen was quoted in *The Times* as saying that he believed that Norma was suffering 'enormous anxiety' as she tried to adapt to her new life. Another London doctor warned that Norma 'could initially feel insecure at official functions and therefore her hosts should try to integrate her into gatherings'. There was another theory that Norma had become overwhelmed by an intense, biting depression that people of particular sensitivity are often prey to at moments of great triumph: a feeling of guilt at not being happy when happiness is what everyone expects.

The *Financial Times* called her 'a puzzle'. The *Independent on Sunday* noted that up until the day her husband had won the leadership election she had somehow managed to remain 'almost invisible'. To the *Sunday Telegraph*, she was simply 'not an easy person to describe'. The problem with Norma was that she didn't appear to fit into any of the conventional slots. She wasn't a Glenys Kinnock sort of wife in that she obviously didn't have any interest in the business of politics and shrank from the limelight, and yet she wasn't quite a cuddly Jane Ashdown; she seemed unapproachable and neurotic by comparison. Perhaps she was just a square peg in a round hole: had she been a Labour Prime Minister's wife, it is interesting to speculate, her homely, unprepossessing manner might well have been regarded as perfectly acceptable.

'I guess Fleet Street always attacks what it doesn't understand, but, to be honest, I did feel a little bit guilty about what I filed,' confesses a reporter responsible for one of the less-than-flatteringly pieces about Norma at the press conference outside No. 10. 'There was just something about her that I found intensely irritating. I suppose it was that she simply didn't appear to be playing the game. She was taking it all so ridiculously seriously.'

Norma did not of course know what it was about her. All she knew was that she had never had a bad word to say about anybody, but here she was being criticised publicly, intemperately, time and again by complete strangers. She did not like this cold, friendless world into which she had stumbled. In it, she felt that she could do nothing right, that there was no place for her, and, desperately, she wanted everything to be like it used to be again. She tried to cling to her old life, her old routine. Like a child embracing a corpse, she could not come to terms with the fact that something had been lost for ever.

The day her husband took office, Norma quietly slipped out of the Horse Guards entrance at No. 10 with Elizabeth and took a taxi to the Royal Opera House to see *The Barber of Seville*. She had been intent on taking up her cheap seats up in the gods among the students and the senior citizens which she had booked months before the leadership imbroglio. It hadn't occurred to her that anybody would see anything amiss.

Of course, the moment that she walked in there was pandemonium. Flustered officials at the opera house swarmed around her.

They were horrified that they had not been notified in advance so that they could have accorded her an official welcome, and then, as one of them said, there were the security implications to be taken into account. When they found out where she was sitting, they couldn't believe it. As they tried to explain, it simply was not done for the Prime Minister's wife to sit in the gods.

With just minutes to go before curtain up, they tried frantically to upgrade her, and, finding it impossible because it was a full house, brought the matter to the attention of Douglas and Judy Hurd who were, by chance, sitting in the Royal Box, guests of Bamber Gascoigne. The party gamely offered to make room for her, but no, Norma was having none of it. She would sit in the seats that she had paid for and there was to be no more fuss. With everybody looking on, she took her seat, and stared resolutely down at those whom she at least considered to be the real stars of the show. It had to be her worst experience in an auditorium since June Bronhill had shouted up at her from the stage of the Coliseum more than a decade ago.

It was clear to Norma that things could not go on as they were. She felt, as she says, 'manoeuvred . . . and nibbled at.' This was not an environment in which she could survive *and* preserve her sanity. She retreated to Finings determined that her life and the lives of her children would get back to normal as quickly as possible. As she made clear to Baroness Blatch, she wasn't going to allow three lives to be ruined just for the sake of one.

Norma got out the Hoover the moment she returned, cleaned the work surfaces and made the hob sparkle. She was determined to rebuild the nest. But there were other things, she found, that she no longer had any control over. In the morning, James found he couldn't take the 8.05 bus to Kimbolton School as normal, the police having stopped him in the driveway and politely told him that they thought it would be a better idea if he accepted a lift in one of their unmarked patrol cars. He argued at first and then there was a look of resignation and some sorrow on his face as he finally bowed to the inevitable and got into the car.

When Norma went shopping at Tesco's, she was aware suddenly that people's eyes were upon her, which made her feel self-conscious and flustered. Worse, when Elizabeth drove out to go to work, she found herself being trailed by a newspaper photographer. When she told her mother what had happened, Norma reached breaking point. They had finally gone too far. She got the name of the paper that the photographer had been working for and – 'like a tigress defending her young', according to the man who witnessed her doing it – she shouted down the telephone at his editor: 'You will not harass my children. Surely to God you must have better things for your employees to do.'

She considered the threat that the cameras posed to the family was insidious. There were a lot of people in London, the image-makers at Conservative Central Office as well as the editors, who would have liked nothing better than for Norma and the children to have become full-time human props in prime ministerial photo-opportunities, but the idea repulsed her. Norma's was a very private life: she hated the idea of it being laid bare for the cameras so that everybody in the country could pass judgement on the way that she and her family lived their lives. They had a *right* to their privacy.

To the surprise of none of her close friends, Norma announced that she was once again going to retain Finings as her base and would go to No. 10 only when necessary. It wasn't just for the sake of the children, it was also, paradoxically, her one way of ensuring that she could occasionally have her husband to herself. As she knew very well, at No. 10 she would have to diary her appointments with him; at Chequers there would invariably be strangers in earshot; and, even in his car, there was always the driver and the man from Special Branch. Finings was her last chance to have any kind of private life with John. It was hard enough to get John's undivided attention even there. The moment he walked through the door, the direct line from Downing Street always seemed to ring. It didn't make a brr-brr noise or a warble, she complained, it just made a constant ring, and she grew to hate the sound of it.

Norma was only the second Prime Minister's wife this century to decide not to live in No. 10 – after Mrs Wilson, who had refused to go back there when her husband won his second General Election, saying that the place made her 'sick with fear'. Few, if any, Prime Ministers' wives appear to have been happy there. Lady Home said that the building had turned her into 'a grass widow'. Lady Churchill admitted: 'I always preferred my own home.' Lady Callaghan said that she found it 'a lonely, impersonal place – I think I only managed to survive by keeping myself busy'. Lady Attlee, asked if she was pleased to be living at the address, snapped back: 'It was the last thing I wanted.' Lady Macmillan kept her time there to a minimum and the staff's most abiding memory of her was that she always seemed to be in a hurry to get back to Birch Grove. And Lady Eden, so briefly in residence, complained that it was a building in which she had never felt able to escape the pressures of her husband's office. She observed memorably that she had always had the feeling that the Suez Canal was flowing through the drawing room.

The problem with No. 10 is that it isn't a home at all but, first and foremost, an office for several hundred people. Its front door opens and shuts an average of one thousand times a day – such was the result of a count initiated by Mrs Wilson in what was clearly a mood of exasperation rather than inquiry. Since the bomb-proof iron gates have gone up at the entrance to Downing Street, a sense of foreboding has pervaded the place, from which the Prime Minister's four-bedroomed flat, on the top floor at the rear of the building, is scant refuge. When the Majors first stayed in it they found that the pale yellow walls and chintz sofa covers introduced by Mrs Thatcher had left it with a cold, clinical feel, the carpet was in need of replacement, and the kitchen, dating from the pre-microwave sixties, was spartan and small, as was the dining room. In the mornings, if the antiquated plumbing didn't wake them up, then the Grenadier Guards, rehearsing for the Trooping of the Colour just outside in Horse Guards, certainly did.

John was himself unperturbed by Norma's decision not to move to No. 10 full-time. 'He has always taken the view that she shouldn't be made to do anything that she doesn't want to on account of his job,' says Barbara Wallis. The press were however less understanding. Several newspapers wondered if Norma had any idea quite how much it was going to cost to guard Finings twenty-four hours a day: one estimate put it as high as £1.5 million a year, a sum which would have to be borne by the county's ratepayers, which had the local MPs grumbling, even if they were Conservatives. They pointed out that had she gone to live in one of the government-owned properties provided for her, the security bill would have been paid by the Home Office.

Others saw it as further evidence that the 'mousey little woman' could not cope. She was running away from No. 10 in terror because she simply wasn't up to it. In the offices of some of the tabloid newspapers, another conclusion was drawn: that because the Prime Minister and his wife had chosen to live apart, there had to be 'another woman'. Teams of reporters were assigned the task of finding this woman and one or two rather unlikely suspects were approached, one of them a lady of not inconsiderable girth, and offered large sums of money to tell all. Norma said she was aware that there were 'unsavoury rumours' circulating and said that she would like to talk to the people who were spreading them 'to put them straight'.

The family were aghast at the suggestion. John's sister Mrs Dessoy says: 'Ever since John had become an MP, he had lived in London and Norma had lived in Huntingdon. There was nothing new in that. It wasn't a story. All sorts of working men only see their wives at weekends. That doesn't destroy a marriage if people go into it for the right reasons. Just because most of the politicians up there in London can't keep it in their trousers during the week, that's no reason to assume that John can't either.'

John was even more annoyed. He told his biographer Bruce

Anderson that if anybody stated in print that he had ever been unfaithful to his wife, he would sue, and he didn't care about the convention that government ministers, let alone the Prime Minister, did not resort to the libel laws. 'Nobody,' he said 'will get away with saying that about me.'

The personal nature of the attacks on the Prime Minister and his wife so early on in an administration are without precedent. As Mrs Dessoy says: 'It would be interesting, wouldn't it, to go through the newspapers from the time that John became Prime Minister, to see how many of the articles which were written about him and Norma were straightforward reports of what they were actually doing and saying, compared to the number which were just mindless gossip, attacks on them as people or all sorts of made-up nonsense based on anonymous sources.' John himself has said that he believed '80 per cent' of the stories being written about him and his wife were at best inaccurate, and, at worst, deliberately intended to wound.

The Majors were clearly a new kind of Tory couple and a lot of people appeared to have some difficulty in accepting them. One Tory grandee observed: 'Just a few decades ago, the only way a couple like that would have made it into No. 10 would have been as housemaid and butler.' There had been previous occupants who had had humble backgrounds, but none of them had adapted so little to their changed circumstances as John and Norma. Their closest friends still live not in the great town houses of Belgravia or the sprawling country estates, but in the two-up, two-downs of Lambeth and Huntingdon. They both still look and sound very much as they had when they first met. Their weakness, as it is their strength, is that they have risen to the pinnacle of the British Establishment without ever having troubled to have become a part of it.

The *Daily Mail*'s diarist Nigel Dempster noted acidly that he has never seen John and Norma at any dances at Chatsworth given by the Duke of Devonshire. And he did not consider it likely that, given the sort of people they were, he would see them there in the future because they simply were not *accepted*. The TV programme *Spitting Image* lampooned the Majors as dull suburbanites, engaging in earnest discussions about the shape of peas, and showing them surrounded by such potent symbols of their class as a Teasmade (Norma had admitted owning one in an interview), a satellite dish and a bottle of tomato ketchup. Roger Law, one of the programme's founding fathers, says: 'John and Norma were a gift for us. The first time I saw them I couldn't quite believe the way that they spoke and acted. I thought they were deliberately parodying themselves, then I realised that they were really like that.'

The former *Daily Telegraph* editor Lord Deedes, a long-time friend of the last Prime Minister's consort and himself an ex-minister, feels that good old-fashioned British snobbery under-laid a lot of the criticism. 'There is a feeling in some quarters, not least among journalists, who have among their number some of the worst snobs in the country, that the Majors were not up to the job socially, that they were a bit common,' he says 'They fell short of their preconceived notion of what a Tory Prime Minister and his wife ought to be like.'

A senior lobby correspondent says he recalled hearing his colleagues guffawing with laughter in the Commons press benches when they heard John refer to something costing 'fifty-five pound' when of course they would have said, having come from the 'right' backgrounds, 'fifty-five *pounds*'. Terry Major-Ball admits he was annoyed about a story which claimed John tucked his shirt into his underpants. 'I mean, is that really *news*?' he wonders. The scorn which John had brought down upon himself and his wife for violating the class system was frequently manifest in the *Daily Telegraph* in the writings of Charles Moore, its old Etonian political commentator, now editor of the *Sunday Telegraph*. Moore, the Young Fogey, and Major, the Classless Man, had had a celebrated confrontation during the leadership election. 'You've been known as quite a shy, retiring man,' Moore had put to him icily. 'People wouldn't say you had Mr Heseltine's star quality or Mr Hurd's presence on the world stage. What is it that *you* can contribute that they don't?' Robert Atkins admits that he had never seen John so distressed as when he came out of that interview. That the attacks continued after his election horrified John, coming as they did from a paper which could traditionally be relied upon to be loyal to a Tory government. John was clear in his own mind about what was behind it all. He told friends that he considered the *Telegraph*'s attacks upon him 'poisonous'.

Baroness Blatch traces some of the criticism back to the 'left-wing intelligentsia' who despised John for appearing to be proud of the fact that he had got so far without any academic qualifications to speak of, and Norma for no other reason than that she was married to him. 'They seriously underestimated both John and Norma,' she says. 'They looked at him and saw this man with this slightly strangled voice and an Adrian Mole view of the world, and they looked at his wife, this little woman who picked up peas from under the table, and they were too prejudiced against them to see anything else.' As a Labour-supporting newspaper, the *Daily Mirror*'s opposition to John was understandable, but as a paper which supposedly spoke up for the working man, its line of attack was not. They too were attacking him for his ordinariness – 'Oooh, look Norma, it's me with lots and lots of famous people,' was how it started off a report about John attending a celebrity fund-raising night for the Conservatives at No. 12 Downing Street.

Some of the opposition was coming from inside as well as outside the party. Mrs Dessoy says: 'There is an element in the Conservative Party which believes that if you are not an Oxford man you cannot possibly be the sort of figure mentally or physically to lead the party. And there are others who are disturbed that, as a Conservative Prime Minister, he is interested in the small man. If he succeeds, that sets a precedent which they don't want to see set.' Among the Tory women, the backbone of the party, eyebrows were being raised too at Norma, as Harvey Thomas, the party's former image guru, has discerned. The

Prime Minister's wife has always been seen as the role model for Tory women throughout the country, and being women often possessed of considerable social aspirations, a great many of them had what Thomas calls 'a problem' with the idea of Norma in that role. 'Now they are perfectly pleasant, these women, and they choose their words carefully,' says Thomas, choosing his own words with some care, 'but they can make somebody *aware* when they don't altogether approve.'

David Mellor was one of many of the Majors' friends enraged by the things people were saying about them. He saw the attacks on them as attacks on ordinary, decent people up and down the land. The criticism of Norma, an innocent bystander in the political arena, he found especially hard to take. As he says: 'If people say that they don't like Norma and the clothes she wears and the way she acts, then the implication is that she and politicians' wives generally should follow the lead of their American counterparts, with their ghastly false hair, false smiles and false everything else – is that what we *really* want?'

At least the Majors derived one advantage from remaining true to their roots and their old friends, even the humble ones: it made it well-nigh impossible for the journalists to find anyone with a bad word to say against them. Maggie Scott says that the journalists who came up to Huntingdon often complained that no one in the town was prepared to say anything of interest about them at all. Everybody would simply trot out the same anodyne comments about the new Prime Minister and his wife being 'a very nice couple' and, eyeing their inquisitors disapprovingly, would go on to talk darkly about the media intrusion in the couple's lives. 'They always seemed to think that we were hiding something about John and Norma,' says Mrs Scott. 'Well, the fact of the matter is they are just two very ordinary, very nice people. It's very inconvenient for the press, I know, but, I'm sorry, that's just the way it is.'

Mrs Scott feels that the personal remarks the press had been making about Norma were beneath contempt, and she then went on to make a personal remark about the hairstyle of the editor of the *Sunday Times*. 'Some people in this country can dole it out, but they never have to take it,' she says. Rosemary Juggins refers to the journalists as 'creatures' and says that when they started gathering around Finings, she had wanted to go out and tell them to leave John and Norma alone. Even Sue Winn, such a kindly-looking lady, admits that she had felt a wicked sense of delight when two cars, both driven by reporters, were involved in a head-on collision on the Stukeley Road.

They had a point, but some of the Majors' friends did seem to be taking it a shade too far: a number seemed to be saying, to all intents and purposes, that if one of their friends had it in mind to be the Prime Minister, then he should be allowed to get on with it in the privacy of his own home and everybody else should simply mind their own business.

However, the protective shield that Norma's friends threw around her enabled her to come to terms with her position in her own time. Her biggest problem when she sat down and looked at the task ahead was that hers was a job which didn't come with a written statement of the terms and conditions. The closest there had been to such a document was an open letter in the *Independent* on 'Being the Wife of the Leader' which Judy Steel had written to Jane Ashdown at the time of the succession in the old Liberal Party in 1988. It was a considered, intelligent analysis which was as relevant to Norma at that point as it had been to Mrs Ashdown.

'I should warn you that the hours of access to your husband will be severely limited,' Mrs Steel wrote. 'Custody of him will have passed out of your hands and into those of the party. Don't expect him back before the small hours, and, if he isn't already an early riser, the demands of the producer of the *Today* programme for instant comments will soon turn him into one.'

As the leader's wife, she cautioned her successor that she too would be expected to perform for the media. 'You may, like me, hate the clicking of cameras . . . but they do matter. You know already that you must hang on every word your husband says in public, because if for one moment your look of enthralment and inspiration drops, that's what they will capture for posterity.' In her dealings with the journalists, Mrs Steel said that it would be necessary for Mrs Ashdown to take care not to say anything that could embarrass her husband, and to insist, every time, on the right to approve copy before agreeing to see anyone. Most of the people who would come to see her, she added, would be from women's magazines, and most of the interviewers would be women. 'I must tell you now, that they won't understand you, or at any rate few of them will. Once they divine your intelligence, they'll be trying to find the frustrated careerist . . . I hope you'll continue to defend a woman's right to be a full-time homemaker . . . Finally, at all costs, avoid journalists such as the one who, among other sneerings, called my loose covers faded (they were precisely six months old).'

As pleasant as such perks as VIP air tickets and Centre Court tickets at Wimbledon might be, Mrs Steel suggested that it was best not to grow too accustomed to them, for they may not last. To this she added that Mrs Ashdown would be well-advised to cancel any engagements that she might have had for the week of the party conference, because she would be expected to be there, at her husband's side, throughout. The sense that Mrs Steel was only too pleased to be handing on the torch came across all too clearly in her next line: 'You can think of David and I motoring along the Loire during that week, enjoying our first September holiday for twelve years.'

Rosemary Juggins knew that Norma was ready to face the world again after a few months when Norma told her, with a wry smile on her face: 'I suppose what makes the prospect of it bearable is the fact that it isn't going to go on forever – and, once it's over, life will have to start getting back to normal again.' She reached an accommodation of sorts with No. 10 whereby she would put herself at their disposal for two days each week. Barbara Wallis, John's constituency secretary, was persuaded to 'run Mrs Major's office' in addition to carrying out her existing responsibilities – a good choice, it was thought, because hers was one of the few faces at No. 10 which would be familiar to Norma, from the Lambeth days. Not a lady to mince her words, Miss Wallis admits that for both Norma and herself the experience turned out to be 'hell on earth'.

A great many people have the impression that the wife of the British Prime Minister, like the wife of the American or the French President, would have at her disposal battalions of secretaries, at least one chauffeur-driven limousine, and a high-flying personal assistant, who would be well up on protocol, diplomatic niceties, and generally adept at keeping his charge well clear of anything that could be politically embarrassing to her husband. It would therefore come as a great surprise to them, as it did to Miss Wallis, that the Prime Minister's wife had only one person to help her: one Barbara Wallis. Miss Wallis realised then that the job of 'running Mrs Major's office' was going to require rather more of her time than she had at first envisaged.

Miss Wallis, an old hand at No. 10 and well acquainted with its often very quaint ways, knew perfectly well that there was no use complaining. The place was, as she says, in chaos after John Major had moved in. The hurried, abrupt departure of Mrs Thatcher meant that the staff hadn't the luxury of a three-week General Election campaign to lay the ground for the new tenants. From the principal private secretary downwards, everybody was making it up as they went along. The Prime Minister's diary, stretching months ahead, was redrawn from scratch because what Mrs Thatcher had wanted to do wasn't necessarily what Mr Major wanted. Then there was the recession, the European issue, the poll tax and a war brewing in the Gulf. The last thing anybody was thinking about in the early days was Mrs Major's working conditions. 'Amid all the confusion,' says Miss Wallis, 'I got the feeling that they had forgotten that the new Prime Minister actually had a wife.'

Norma muddled through as best she could. One of her early luncheon companions, Judy Hurd, says that when she met her she gave the impression of a woman who was 'still finding her feet . . . She needed time'. She also sensed that Norma didn't like the feeling of not being in control. Norma wondered whether even Mrs Heseltine would have done any better in her shoes. As Norma told Nesta Wyn Ellis: 'Anne Heseltine might not have found it quite as easy as everybody was saying she would.'

Norma knew that a General Election was not far off and saw no point in agonising too much about the nature of her role until the British people had decided whether they wanted her husband to be anything more than a caretaker at No. 10. She would work from home whenever she could – even the Herculean task of sending out the Prime Minister's personal Christmas cards was undertaken largely from Finings (at the local post office they still talk about the day when Mrs Major turned up and asked for 500 stamps as if it was the most ordinary thing in the world). Olive Baddeley, surprised to hear that she was doing the job on her own, came round to help, and found her sitting at her word processor surrounded by cards neatly stacked in different piles – with different salutations appropriate to the status of the recipient.

During her two days in London, Norma averaged four engagements a day and went to one evening function. The engagements were kept as low profile as possible because it was still a great ordeal for her to be the focus of attention. Mrs Baddeley had tried vainly to instil in Norma some sense of her new position: 'You must remember that people are more afraid of meeting you these days than you are of meeting them,' she told her. Sandra Barwick, a journalist from the *Independent* who watched Norma at one of her early appearances – at a fairly innocuous press conference to launch a sponsored fitness programme – was still saddened by what she saw. She wrote: 'I have never seen a woman in the public eye who shrank from it with quite such intensity of feeling, and this, a dozen years after her husband's first election success. The heart sinks at how many more such events she must be enduring.'

The relationship between Norma and the press remained at best prickly. Initially, Miss Wallis says that Norma gave almost every journalist who requested an interview the benefit of the doubt, but a run of hostile articles taught her to be more selective. In the company of journalists, Norma began to choose her words with a greater care than ever before. Whereas she had been quoted in the past as saying – to the *Shropshire Magazine*, for instance – that her father had been killed 'in action' during the Second World War, she now saw how important it was to make it clear that he had died just after VE-Day in an accident. As the Prime Minister's wife, she knew very well that whatever she said could and probably would be checked and double-checked.

At other times, with the best of intentions, she did let the side down. After rumours began circulating that her husband's health was suffering as a result of his heavy workload, she gave an interview to the *Cambridge Evening News* with the specific intention of assuring the public that there was nothing to worry about. She inadvertently fanned the flames by saying in passing that she wished he would ease up – and that of course was the one comment the national papers picked up. The next day she made matters worse still by saying that her husband and herself were 'limping' towards the next public holiday. A number of commentators, such as Chris Moncrieff, the Press Association's veteran political editor, concluded that Norma had no political instinct whatsoever. 'She just seemed to say whatever was on her mind – and in the environment in which she operated, that was, of course, a very dangerous tendency,' he says.

That is not to say that Norma did not have a very specific idea of how she herself wished to be seen: essentially as a loyal and supportive wife to John. The unkind comments about her clothes, her demeanour, even her personality, paled into insignificance beside anything that appeared to contradict that one vital point. One of John's biographers, Nesta Wyn Ellis, was bemused when Norma objected to a seemingly harmless passage in her book that said he had a liking for junk food. It so happens that John *does* like junk food, but it was of course the implication that Norma didn't bother to cook proper food for him, to her so integral a part of being a good wife, that she found so objectionable. (On the question of whether Norma is a good cook her friends are, incidentally, split down the middle. Olive Baddeley says that the answer is definitely no – 'She hates going into the kitchen' – whereas Ian Cameron Black strenuously puts the case for the defence, citing as evidence her 'exquisite crackling and roast potatoes'. For her part, Norma has admitted: 'I don't like cooking, partly because the children have never been interested in food and John is away so much. You tend to get out of practice.')

Norma's image appeared to be of concern to Conservative Central Office too. Given her remarks in the past about her wariness of the image-makers, it was hard to believe that it was her idea to call in the make-up expert Barbara Daly, a woman held in high esteem in Smith Square for the running repairs she was able to effect on Mrs Thatcher during her final years in office. Ms Daly says diplomatically that all she knows is that the initial call came from Norma herself and she was not privy to any discussions which might have preceded it.

Ms Daly gave Norma 'a softer look, which made the most of her eyes, her best feature'. For her hair, she ordered her to forsake the local hairdressers at Huntingdon and go instead to Ian Denson who worked at John Frieda, one of the more fashionable West End salons. When the twenty-six-year-old stylist asked Norma what look she was striving for, she was reported to have replied: 'I don't want to appear like I have just been got hold of.' He says he realised from the outset that his new client was very much a 'wash and go' kind of a lady. He cut her hair a little shorter, and, to use one of the splendid euphemisms of his trade, introduced a little 'warmth'. Norma emerged the other side of Daly and Denson's powder puffs and colorants looking much the same, but for a curious, artificial kind of glow, which is most commonly associated with American women of a certain age who frequent the health clubs of some of the pricier hotels. Whatever else it was, it was not the Norma that John had fallen in love with or the children had called mother. Terry Major-Ball, looking at some of the 'glamour' pictures she did, says he wondered if he was not alone in preferring 'the old Norma'.

Norma is not an unattractive woman, but she is not, as she knows very well, 'beautiful' in the conventional sense, so she was taken aback rather than flattered when men started using the word to describe her. Olive Baddeley says that she used to sense her 'curling up inside herself' when someone suddenly began to heap praise upon her, particularly in public. As Norma also knew only too well, she was suddenly considered beautiful for no other reason than that she was the Prime Minister's wife. If she had still been married to a councillor, these people wouldn't have been giving her a second glance. She was embarrassed more for them than herself.

The sense of unreality that was pervading her life began to worry her. There she was watching *Inspector Morse* at Finings as real-life inspectors wandered around her garden outside. Sitting in a Range Rover on the Balmoral Estate, she suddenly had to pinch herself because she was actually chatting to the Queen. Afterwards she told Derek Oakley, Barbara Wallis's husband, that she had said to herself: 'Norma, for God's sake, that's the *Queen* you're talking to.' As a child she had *dreamt* of meeting the Queen. And then there was John about to send thousands of British servicemen to risk their lives against Saddam Hussein's army, and she was worrying about whether he would be able to carve the turkey for the family on Christmas Day.

Norma consciously divided what happened to her as the Prime Minister's wife from what she considered 'real life' which was, to all intents and purposes, what took place at Finings. Friends such as Sue Winn says she felt that when she spoke to them she was to some extent 'playing along with the act'. As Mrs Winn says: 'I would always make a point of keeping the conversation to ordinary things such as her hair or how Elizabeth was getting on, because that was what she seemed to want me to do. She would never start talking about some of the glamorous things that she had been doing, such as seeing George and Barbara Bush at Camp David, because she knew that it would immediately put a barrier between us.' Norma had told David Mellor's wife Judy that she hated the idea of being seen as a name-dropper: 'If I went around saying, "Of course when I was at Buckingham Palace, the Queen said to me . . . " it could be misinterpreted.' 'She realises,' says David Mellor, 'that, as far as she is concerned, all this Prime Minister stuff is transitory, and it is silly to take it too seriously.'

Andrew Thomson recalls that when Norma went out to dinner after John became Prime Minister, everybody sitting around her tended to expect her to be the life and soul of the party. 'They would want her to talk about all the famous people she had been meeting and the exciting things she had been doing, but Norma would never do that. It is just not her way. She is not and never has been a performer. It might seem strange, but she is a woman who is genuinely embarrassed by success.'

It was, however, becoming more and more of an uphill struggle for her to preserve the status quo at Finings. Sunday lunch for all the family used to be sacrosanct, but, she admitted, it was now an all too rare occurrence. She had a dream, she confided, just to sit down in front of the television set with John to watch a Peter Sellers film with a take-away curry on their laps. For her, the simplest pleasures had suddenly taken on a special lustre.

On the other side of the looking glass, Norma's 'pretend life' was becoming ever more eventful. She accompanied John to Maine to stay with George and Barbara Bush at their holiday home. She loved Barbara, but was not quite so keen on George – 'a bit full of himself', she confided to a friend when she got back. Then there was a lightning tour of Moscow (she liked Gorbachov, she said), Beijing and Hong Kong, leaving on a Sunday night and returning the following Friday. The split-second scheduling of these tours annoyed her intensely: her minders had wanted her to see the Peto Institute for handicapped children in Hungary in twenty minutes, imagining that she would only want to use it for the purposes of a quick photo-opportunity. She negotiated them up to three-quarters of an hour, and even that, she felt, wasn't long enough to get a proper insight. When she got back to Britain, feeling a bit queasy after all the pills which she had had to take for her travel sickness, she went on to Balmoral with her husband, where the Queen and Prince Philip entertained them at their famous annual barbecue on the moors. Philip did the cooking – Norma was especially fond of his sausages – and afterwards she helped clear up. In her room that night, a small ornament caught her eye. She turned it over and found, to her delight, that it was inscribed with the words 'A gift from the people of Huntingdon'. She liked to think that the Queen had put it there to make her feel at home.

In London, Norma's down-to-earth outlook appeared quaint, even risible to many of the people who came across her. At No. 10 she made almost all her telephone calls personally. She would also be the first to pick up a phone when she heard it ringing, which had a number of hapless callers wondering if the woman at the other end of the line was spoofing them. 'Oh yes, and I am John,' they would say. A newspaper interviewer asked Norma about Chequers, the Prime Minister's country home in Buckinghamshire. 'Oh yes, Chequers,' she said, as if it had slipped her mind. 'I'm not sure how we're going to fit Chequers in. I am afraid I would not know where to start when it came to running a stately home.' Others laughed at the way she refused to have a home help at Finings for more than three hours a week and still made the Prime Minister bring his dirty washing home for her to attend to at weekends. Then there was the occasion she alighted from a plane at Heathrow after a trip to Canada, clasping a Tower Records carrier bag.

When she went out to have lunch in Covent Garden with her friend Carole Stone, the former *Any Questions?* producer, she arrived on the Piccadilly line. 'I persuaded her to take a taxi back, but only after she had protested vigorously,' says a bemused Ms Stone. 'She kept saying how she wanted to keep her life ordinary.' Again after a meeting with Lord Rix at Mencap, she asked where the nearest Tube was. 'Oh, don't worry, love,' Rix told her hastily, 'I'll give you a lift.' At parties, she always hesitated to introduce herself – 'I'm Norma Major' – for fear that people might ask 'Who?' Then there was the time at the hairdresser's when she mentioned to Ian Denson that she had bought a hat at John Lewis's that she wasn't very happy with and she wondered if he thought they might be prepared to change it for her. 'That was so like her,' says Denson.

At No. 10, Norma had established a routine, arriving on Thursday mornings and collecting her correspondence from Miss Wallis, which she would then take upstairs to attend to in the Prime Minister's private quarters. She received about a hundred letters a week from a very varied range of people. Many wanted her personally to bring their problems to her husband's attention, which she would always politely decline to do, suggesting that they contact their local MP instead. Some wanted to help her. Two youngsters who had heard of her interest in raising money for Mencap held a table-top sale outside their home and raised £15, which they sent her, together with a picture of themselves, which touched her greatly. Barbara Kent of the Wagstaff Society wrote to her to inquire if she would like to investigate her family's origins – a service she declined. Some of the other letters were very sad, and affected her greatly, and their writers generally had to be pointed in the direction of the Samaritans or skilled psychiatric help. She got occasional letters from perverts and a little hate mail, always unsigned, which Miss Wallis would intercept and put in the bin. Others were from well-wishers – almost always women – telling her that they liked her the way she was and she wasn't to take any notice of what the press were saying. There was one in particular which cheered her up. Lady Wilson, the wife of the former Labour Prime Minister Harold Wilson, wrote to say that she knew what she was going through. She said that she had never been happy at No. 10 herself – 'I never felt like I was me when I was there' – but she urged her to try to make the best of a bad lot. She advised her to think again about Chequers – it had always been a source of great comfort to her.

Miss Wallis got to know Norma very well during the period that they worked together and came to respect her greatly for her sense of duty, her grace under pressure and her courage. And so it used to irritate Miss Wallis all the more the way that Norma was treated by some of the people who worked at No. 10. It was always assumed that she would be at certain functions, but nobody ever thought to tell her the dates. The Prime Minister's diary was circulated to just about everyone in the building except Norma, who was expected to know what was going on by what Miss Wallis imagined was 'some process of osmosis'. When Boris Yeltsin made his hastily arranged visit to No. 10 shortly after John became Prime Minister, she remembered them coming to Norma at the last minute and telling her to go downstairs to receive him. When she asked them what they wanted her to do, they said that she would just have to 'play it by ear'. She was left nervously pacing the reception area for an hour and a half until Yeltsin, whose plane had been delayed in fog, finally arrived.

It was very much a feeling of 'them' and 'us' in Mrs Major's office. Miss Wallis speaks with scorn of the male-dominated, public-school environment in which they had to operate. Nobody had ever tried to push the last Prime Minister's consort around, but then, as Miss Wallis pointed out, *he* was a man. Among most of the civil servants, ministers' wives, even the Prime Minister's wife, were still considered little more than chattels. Few deigned to talk to either Norma or Miss Wallis and the two women had to learn by trial and error. It was three months after they had started when Miss Wallis casually mentioned that Norma had agreed to officiate at a school awards ceremony. 'Have you checked it out with the Education Department?' a civil servant inquired. Miss Wallis shook her head. 'My dear woman,' he replied, 'for all you know the wretched place could be scheduled for closure. In future, you mustn't agree to anything before checking it out with the relevant department.' It was the same with security. None of them had thought to mention that Norma was supposed to keep Special Branch informed of her movements. It was only when she had slipped out for a private lunch one day and the detectives were running all over the place yelling that they had lost the Prime Minister's wife that this matter too was rectified.

There were days, Miss Wallis says, when things did get too much for Norma, but, typically, it never occurred to her to bring her problems at No. 10 to the attention of her husband. She always used to say that he had quite enough on his mind as it was. After three months, and pretty close to breaking point herself, Miss Wallis submitted a memo to the principal private secretary in which she complained that 'it's absolutely ludicrous to expect a modern Prime Minister's wife to function effectively in these circumstances' and called on him at least to provide her with a car and secretarial assistance. Miss Wallis had to wait three months for a reply, six months for a secretary, and a year for a pool car (coming on condition that it be used only to take Mrs Major to and from official engagements, otherwise she would be billed). Between them, Miss Wallis and Norma managed to establish at least some official guidelines regarding what was required of the Prime Minister's wife, doing it on some days when it looked as if the first person to benefit from all their hard work would be Glenys Kinnock.

Norma never impressed Miss Wallis more than on the morning when she was chatting to her on the telephone from Finings and she heard what sounded like a terrific thunderclap in the background.

'What the hell was that?' Norma asked.

'I think it was a bomb,' Miss Wallis replied. 'Hang on and I'll go and find out what's happened.'

Norma was left holding the telephone for ten agonisingly long minutes.

'It's all right,' Miss Wallis finally said, gasping. 'John is fine. Nobody has been hurt.'

'Thank God,' said Norma.

Just hours after the IRA's audacious mortar bomb attack on Downing Street, Norma was in Huntingdon High Street, starting a string of pancake races, as planned. 'That was so like Norma,' says Miss Wallis. 'She just said to me that she felt it was important to carry on as normal.' Some days later Norma quietly admitted to Baroness Blatch that she had been 'numbed' by what had happened. The threat of an assassination attempt on her husband was something that had preyed on her mind ever since he was appointed Foreign Secretary. Throughout the war with Iraq, she had been on tenterhooks, fearing a sniper attack on John. At that moment, however, she hadn't perceived any danger, and had always felt comfortable while John was in Whitehall, because she had assumed that was the one place where he would be safe.

Wives of politicians who have been victim to assassination attempts while they have not been around, such as Nancy Reagan, have often felt profound guilt, and since become virtually inseparable from their husbands. That was not Norma's response. Her desire to spend as little time as possible at No. 10 remained just as strong. It still is. After she completes her last appointment there, even if it is a dinner which has gone on until midnight, she always gets into her car and drive straight home rather than spend another unnecessary moment. Olive Baddeley says that she has told her she worries about her on the roads so late at night. Norma replied that, alone in the car those evenings, it was the one time she had to think, and listen to music.

The advantage of packing Norma's diary so full during the

early months of John's premiership was that she lunged from one trauma to another so quickly that she didn't have much time to dwell on any of them. The Conservative Party Conference in Blackpool struck her as such a hideous prospect that she could only face going there in the company of her old friend Maggie Scott. Mrs Scott's role there was simply as 'a friendly face' – to reassure, encourage, console and, as much as possible, keep her away from the press, who were, Mrs Scott admits, making Norma depressed. Reporters say that there was a look of terror on Norma's face every time she had to leave her hotel room. The one occasion that she dutifully submitted herself to the cameras was when she was wearing a dull bottle-green suit which exactly matched the potted plants she posed against. She was so perfectly camouflaged, one newspaper noted, that the only thing visible was 'her pale, pinched face and startled brown eyes'.

Norma felt the need to call in a friend again when she was hosting a reception at No. 10 for people who cared for handicapped friends and relatives. Ian Cameron Black says that she phoned him and said she couldn't face it on her own. 'There will be people there who will be dying,' she told him. 'I don't know if I am going to be able to look at them.' On the day, Cameron Black says that she rose to the occasion magnificently, even though it began with a crisis. One of the guests, Heather Strudwick, a lady confined to an iron lung since she developed polio in 1957, found that her machine would not fit into the lift to take her up to the first-floor drawing room where the reception was being held. It was the first occasion that she had been out of her home in Colchester for years and the look of disappointment on her face was heart-rending. Norma, who had been watching the scene from the landing, hurried down the stairs and assured Heather that the reception would not be starting without her. If necessary, she said, she would have the whole event transferred to No. 11 Downing Street, where there was a suitable reception area on the ground floor.

Norma summoned four policemen to try to carry Heather up

the stairs in her cumbersome iron lung. It turned out to be a precarious operation. and. once they were past the point of no return, Heather admits that she found it terrifying. As she says: 'I probably wouldn't have made it had it not been for Mrs Major fixing me with her eyes at the top of the stairs and saying: 'Don't worry, Heather, you're nearly there, you're going to be all right.' I felt that I could trust Mrs Major. When she told me I was going to make it, I believed her.' Heather did indeed make it to the top, with her sister, Mrs Patricia Crittenden, who cared for her, not far behind. Mrs Crittenden recalls: 'Mrs Major made us feel as if we were among friends. On these official sort of occasions, people so often look the other way when they see someone who is very handicapped and tend to treat him or her as an object rather than a human being. From the moment Mrs Major saw Heather, she treated her in the way people usually only treat her after they have known her for some years.' After the speeches, Norma gave the two of them an impromptu tour of the first floor of No. 10 and supervised Heather's descent. The police officers carrying her inadvertently knocked three portraits of former prime ministers off the wall. Heather looked up to Norma and quipped: 'There can't be many people who can say that they have brought down three prime ministers in one day!' When all her guests had gone, Norma turned round to Cameron Black and said: 'Wasn't that a lovely event, weren't they lovely people?'

The Commonwealth Summit in Harare turned out to be more of a strain for Norma. Chris Moncrieff, the Press Association's political editor, got the impression that she wasn't too well. 'She seemed nervous and unhappy throughout,' he says. He felt that some members of the press corps covering the event treated her appallingly, asking her questions about policy matters and then openly scoffing at her predictably simplistic answers. 'They had no business asking her questions like that,' says Moncrieff. 'The fact that she happens to be married to the Prime Minister is no qualification per se for her to answer them.' He recalls that John appeared very concerned for her as they walked along the path overlooking Victoria Falls. He lost her momentarily in the crowd, and came back looking for her.

After most of the reporters had dispersed, she had a chat with Nick Davies, then the *Daily Mirror*'s foreign editor, on her way back to the hotel. He suggested that in the evening she should take John for a stroll along the Falls by moonlight because it was one of the most romantic places in the world. 'I'm afraid my husband would be impervious to it,' she replied dolefully. 'He's quite impervious to anything like that.' As it was, she found herself at a banquet that evening trying desperately hard to make conversation with a deaf old man who sat beside her whom she assumed to be Malawi's ageing dictator, Dr Hastings Banda. 'I kept thinking to myself, "I suppose I have got the right man haven't I?"' she told Sue Winn when she got back.

Norma's single greatest challenge of the year was playing hostess to the wives of the world leaders attending the G7 economic summit in London. She had to escort them on a variety of outings deemed appropriate for women by the Foreign Office (and frivolous and patronising by Danielle Mitterrand, who boycotted most of them). There was a sight-seeing trip down the Thames, a tour of Kew Gardens, dinner with the royals, a night out to see the musical *Carmen Jones*, and a visit to Chequers where, according to Miss Wallis, they all had a riotous time, a real girls' day out. There was also the odd hospital visit just to assure the voters back home that it was not all fun and games.

Norma's lack of self-confidence remained the problem. Sitting in a coach at Kew Gardens for what seemed like an eternity, all the wives found themselves waiting for their hostess to stand up and take the lead. Finally Barbara Bush broke the impasse and declared: 'Come on, girls, *one* of us is going to have to make a move, so it might as well be me.' It was of course Norma's misfortune to have to hold her own among one of the most accomplished generations of leaders' wives in living memory. Looking at the other women and what they had come through it was difficult not to be struck by quite how different Norma was.

There was Mrs Bush, America's extraordinarily popular 'grand-mother' figure, whom commentators spoke of as her husband's greatest political asset; Raisa Gorbachov, a former university professor, who met her roughneck husband at Moscow University and took him by the scruff of the neck and trained him to be a president; glamorous Mila Mulroney, credited with keeping her husband from turning to the bottle after he lost his first leadership bid fifteen years earlier; and Danielle Mitterrand, sophisticated, intellectual, more popular in France than her husband, and considered to be more of a Socialist than he ever was.

And what was there for the journalists covering the event to say about Norma? One put it like this: 'Every upward step her husband has taken in his career has mortified her, she hates to leave her home, and she numbers bell-ringing among her hobbies.' It was a harsh assessment. Norma was not the most glamorous and assured of the wives – it was generally agreed that Mila Mulroney had earned that distinction – but she had managed to hold on to some things a lot of them might have wished they still had: a sense of what was important, two well-adjusted children, and some real friends who would still be around long after her husband had left office.

It might not perhaps have been apparent to a foreign journalist that there was also a sound political reason for Norma to spend time at her home. She was unique among the wives at the summit in that her husband had a constituency to look after, and, increasingly since he entered No. 10, it was her duty to represent him there.

Hardly a week went by without Norma popping up at a variety of events in Huntingdon. The school visits, the cocktail circuit, standing in for her husband at a party to celebrate his first anniversary as Prime Minister, even setting light to thousands of pounds' worth of illegal drugs as a stunt for the local police force – she seemed to be everywhere. John's agent Peter Brown said that the people up in London who thought that she only went back to Huntingdon to rest and look after her family were living in cloud cuckoo land.

It was rare for Norma ever to pull out of commitments in the constituency. She turned up on one occasion at an event for the Cambridgeshire Family Health Services Association so ill that her friend Maggie Scott, the Association's chairwoman, took one look at her and drove her home, insisting that she got some rest. Another time she brought forward, without explanation, a visit to a school in Wilburton. It so happened that she had good reason for doing that too. It would have clashed with a General Election campaign. And she knew that, unlike the leadership contest, she wouldn't be able to sit that one out at Finings. Central Office wouldn't stand for that – and neither would the press.

CHAPTER 6

Battle of the First Ladies

WITH VERY LITTLE happening centre stage during the 1992 General Election campaign, a lot of news editors desperately sought a sideshow which would hold their readers' attention. One of the most promising of these looked like being what the *Today* newspaper dubbed the Battle of the First Ladies.

Ever more banal lists started appearing in all the tabloids, giving marks out of ten for the couture, coiffure and campaigning styles of the wives of the three contenders: Norma Major, Glenys Kinnock and Jane Ashdown. Even the broadsheets got caught up in it, carrying long, earnest features which pondered the conundrum of the role of the modern statesman's wife.

Journalists of the old school such as Lord Deedes were dismayed by the vast acres of newsprint being devoted to the women. Their views, with the greatest respect, were really neither here nor there. It was, he feels, a sad reflection on the new order in Fleet Street that space which could have been used for serious analyses of the issues was being wilfully squandered on so frivolous an exercise.

Lady Callaghan, the last Prime Minister's wife, says that she had been all but forgotten during her husband's election campaigns; she would go along to hear Jim speak when she felt like it, she recalls, often travelling separately to his meetings by Tube. She wore whatever she happened to have on at the time, which didn't matter because she was seldom, if ever, photographed, and, had her party had such a fellow as 'campaign manager' in those days – she honestly isn't sure – then she is pleased to say that he had never thought it necessary to introduce himself to her.

Twelve years on, the press and the political parties had entered into an unholy alliance which made the job of being married to a party leader during an election campaign very much less palatable. The American-style approach to the business of campaigning which the parties had lately embraced meant that image was suddenly all-important. A vital part of this image for both of the main candidates was to be seen as a good family man, and, accordingly, their respective campaign managers had to make it their business to acquaint the electorate with their man's missus.

Harvey Thomas, the Conservative Party's former director of presentation and promotion, who advised Norma on an unofficial basis during the General Election campaign, proffers myriad reasons why he considers it so important for today's prime ministerial hopeful to have a high-profile wife. In this age of equality, it is important that his marriage is seen to be a partnership. There are sound aesthetic grounds in that the wife's presence tends to make for better television or better photographs. And then there is the old argument that if he wants to get the vote of the ordinary man, he has first to portray himself as an ordinary man. Part of this is demonstrating that he knows what it is like to support a family, that he believes in family values, and that he is – 'let's face it,' says Thomas – a heterosexual. A wife by his side was, he contends, clear evidence of all three attributes.

Only Des Wilson, the Liberal Democrats' plain-speaking campaign manager, is prepared to reject these words as sophistry. He believes that the real reason why the two main parties put such emphasis on their leaders' wives during the '92 campaign was because they were uncomfortably aware that their leaders were themselves such insipid characters. Throughout the campaign, Wilson says he never wasted any time worrying about how best to project his candidate as a man of the people because he did not think that there was any doubt in anybody's mind that he was. And, he adds wryly, he certainly never felt it necessary to prove that *his* man was a heterosexual.

In the event, the three wives proved quite a novelty act, but, despite the best efforts of a great many journalists, they showed little inclination to follow the example of their counterparts across the Atlantic and start slugging it out among themselves. Worse, Norma Major, Glenys Kinnock and Jane Ashdown acted as if they genuinely got along.

It so happened that it was more than just an act. Norma had often chatted to both Mrs Kinnock and Mrs Ashdown at Westminster functions and all three had got to know and respect each other. They were three intelligent, amiable women: there was no reason why they shouldn't get on. There was of course an etiquette to be observed when they got together. It wasn't done to talk about political matters, allude to current news stories which were critical of any of their husbands, and they shouldn't complain about the lack of time that they had with their husbands, because, as Mrs Ashdown says, that could be taken as read. Their conversations were none the less always frank and open. Very much the new girl, Norma would turn to the wives of her husband's two principal antagonists for advice and moral support. To her it was the most natural thing in the world to do: she was after all coming up to hurdles for the first time which they had already had to find ways of getting over.

Norma was still angry at a lot of things which were happening to her and her family, whereas Mrs Kinnock and Mrs Ashdown often seemed resigned to them as occupational hazards. They had quite a debate once on the subject of press intrusion into their children's lives when Norma turned up at a drinks party incandescent with rage after discovering that a reporter had been trying to find out how James had been doing at school. It didn't seem right to her that the children should ever have to be dragged into it. Mrs Kinnock replied calmly that she understood her anger: it so happened that far from just making idle inquiries about her son Stephen, reporters were actually offering cash to his fellow students at Cambridge specifically to come up with some dirt on him. For certain newspapers, she said, the children of politicians were fair game. Mrs Kinnock said that she believed that the answer was legislation to curb the press. 'It is not sufficient to feel bitter about what the press do during election campaigns. They seem to feel that at such times using any kind of scurrilous attack is acceptable, even if it has no foundation in truth, because it is the initial impact that matters.'

Norma said that on that point they were certainly agreed. Mrs Ashdown, however, demurred. She told them that she found the idea of any journalist prying into her children's lives just as offensive, but legislation was a dangerously blunt tool to use against it. Newspaper readers, for a start, ought to be encouraged to be more responsible — she took the *Guardian* and the *Sunday Times* and made it a rule never to buy a paper out of curiosity after some new scandal had broken.

The exchanges between the three women were always frank and lively. By simply talking such things through, realising that they were not alone in their predicament, they all usually went away feeling a little better about the world. Mrs Ashdown says it was therapeutic. People who saw them chatting away so amicably — MPs among them — would often come up and make the same, somewhat patronising remark: 'How much more civilised Parliament would be if you all had your husbands' jobs.'

During the campaign, the wives occasionally had to answer the same questions from journalists and their replies said a lot about their different personalities. They were asked if they ever had rows with their husbands — Mrs Ashdown replied: 'Yes, but not often. I'm very slow to lose my temper, but, once it's gone, that's it. My husband is the same and whichever of us is stamping and yelling, the other tends to go quiet.' Mrs Kinnock: 'No. People think that we do because we are both volatile, but mostly we just end up laughing about things.' And Norma: 'I suppose we do disagree occasionally, but he's usually right.' Asked what they imagined their first words to their respective husbands would be on the day after the election, Mrs Ashdown replied: 'Let's go on holiday. You need a rest.' Mrs Kinnock: 'We made it.' And Norma: 'This is the first day of the rest of our lives.'

Mrs Kinnock wanted victory for her husband more than anything in the world. He had worked harder and longer for it, she felt, than any other man in the race, and she had no doubt that he was ready for it. Mrs Ashdown said that she wanted it both ways – on the one hand, she wanted to see her husband win, but on the other, she also wanted to preserve her personal privacy and her family life which she knew would not be possible if her husband won.

Norma went into the General Election telling everybody that she would love to see her husband installed in No. 10 in his own right, but to a lot of the people the words sounded rehearsed and hollow. The Press Association's Sally Weale, who interviewed her at the beginning of the campaign, remarks: 'Whatever she said, one could not help feeling that in her heart of hearts she would have preferred to return to the days of relative anonymity as a constituency wife.'

Temperamentally Mrs Ashdown had more in common with Norma than Mrs Kinnock. She too hadn't the confidence to get up and make speeches, very obviously put the family at the top of her list of priorities, and preferred the quiet life at her cottage near Yeovil to the showy Westminster scene. Her family background, like Norma's, was staunchly Conservative, even if she had subsequently changed course. Mrs Ashdown could find it within herself to hate political parties, she notes, but never the people involved. Of Norma, she says: 'She is a lovely person. She is one of those people who would be incapable of being cruel to anyone. My husband says that she has an inner grace and I think that's very true.'

Mrs Ashdown got on well with Norma and Mrs Kinnock because she could appreciate the role that fate had played in casting them as rivals in that year's General Election: 'I married a Marine thirty years ago. Glenys married a lad she had met at university twenty-five years ago. And Norma married a local councillor twenty-two years ago. None of us actually *chose* to be in the positions that we found ourselves.'

Remembering how it had been for her after her husband's election to the party leadership in 1988, Mrs Ashdown says that she empathised strongly with Norma. At the time everybody had wanted to interview her and take her picture. At first she had found it very flattering, but it didn't take long for her to realise that she was simply being used. It was a disconcerting moment when it suddenly struck her that the reporters who were coming to see her, and being so nice to her, were doing so not because they wanted to but because it was their job. She felt that a lot of the things which were written about her were unfair. The cheap cracks about the furnishings she had chosen in her home made her blood boil, but Paddy would always say to her that she shouldn't complain, that she should never give them the satisfaction of knowing that they had got to her. So she says that she would just get angry and stamp around in the privacy of her own home, which wasn't nearly so satisfying.

At her husband's first conference as leader of the Liberal Democrats, Mrs Ashdown surprised a lot of people when she said that she was not going to sit next to him on the platform. She considered herself just an ordinary member of the party and didn't see any reason why there should be anything to separate her from the other members. There were party officials who were worried that the public might think that she was not being supportive of her husband, but her view prevailed. 'In any case I'm just not the sort of political wife who can gaze up at my husband in awe,' she says. 'I am incapable of looking at him like that.'

Mrs Ashdown was irritated by the way that she was treated by the press: all the sexist questions about her hair and her make-up, nobody ever seemed to be asking her about anything important. Almost always she seemed to get some gormless young girl from the women's pages, seldom, if ever, a serious news reporter. 'But then,' she says, thinking out loud, 'they treated Denis Thatcher as a bit of a joke too, so perhaps it isn't just sexism, perhaps it is more complicated than that. They seem to feel a need to snipe at anybody who dares to be married or related to a person in power. Maybe it's because they want to get at our husbands or wives by attacking us, or maybe they just think that we have to be ridiculous to marry people like that.'

Mrs Ashdown was worried, as Norma was, about what effects her husband's career would have on her children, Kate and Simon, but they were both in their twenties by the time Paddy was elected leader of the party and mercifully past the most vulnerable phase in their lives. Simon's girlfriend was a bit concerned when she discovered who his father was, but she did overcome it, and consented when he proposed to her. Her children were lucky in that they both had what she called 'great in-built crap detectors' – they were able to see through people who wished to use them for their own ends. Mrs Ashdown feels that she, Mrs Kinnock and Norma have been very, very lucky that their children have all turned out so well. She is conscious of the fact that the slightest problem – psychological, emotional, sexual, whatever – is always grotesquely magnified for children unlucky enough to have a political leader as their father.

Of the three wives, Mrs Ashdown was able to go into the campaign in the most relaxed frame of mind. It had been agreed, long before the election was called, that she would be of most use staying put in Yeovil for the duration, rather than trailing behind her husband with what she calls 'a fixed grin and aching feet'. In a small party, they couldn't even afford to take the leader's seat for granted and accordingly her role canvassing in the constituency on his behalf was seen as crucial.

If her husband did win the General Election, Mrs Ashdown said that she would move into No. 10 with him, but dutifully rather than enthusiastically. She added the rider that had she still had a child at school, as Norma had, she would definitely have stayed at home. She said that she did not relish, any more than Norma, the commitments or the media attention which came with the job of being the Prime Minister's wife. As for how she felt she could use the role most constructively, she cheerfully admitted that she hadn't given the matter a moment's thought. Given the electoral system in the country, she always knew that it would be a 'bloody miracle' if her husband won the national vote, but she knew too that, almost irrespective of the result, it would be unlikely that the party would dump him. Mrs Kinnock and Norma, on the other hand, were playing for higher stakes – both their husbands were fighting for their political lives.

Glenys Kinnock said that if her husband won she would go to live with him in No. 10 full-time and would be proud to do so. She said that she wanted to use the role of Prime Minister's wife to benefit the various charities and humanitarian organisations that she was connected with, but she would not, she was at pains to point out, use it to engage in any political activity or seek to influence her husband on matters of policy. 'It is a great fallacy that I go around making speeches for the Labour Party,' she said. 'I never have – because I have always been conscious of the fact that I haven't been elected. Those speeches I have made have always been on behalf of organisations that I have an active interest in myself.'

On the face of it, Mrs Kinnock appeared to have little in common with the other two wives. An accomplished public speaker, confident, glamorous, eager to have her say on national issues in her own spheres of activity, she seemed as different from them as scarlet designer suits were from woolly cardigans.

But in the early days she had found it just as difficult to adjust to the role of politician's wife. She was just as lonely and miserable as they were when her husband was first elected as the MP for Bedwellty in South Wales and she was left to bring up her children on her own in the family home. She found it no easier when her husband was elected to the leadership of his party in 1983. She told friends at the time that she was 'panic-stricken' at the thought of the inevitable pressures that lay ahead and was fiercely protective towards her children – Stephen, then thirteen, and Rachel, eleven. She too shunned the press and was aghast when a photographer from the *Daily Express* thought it worthwhile photographing her as she unloaded her car after a trip to Sainsbury's the day before her husband's election. 'I don't see how Neil will ever be able to help me with the shopping again,' she said dolefully.

It soon became clear, however, that she did not subscribe to the view that because she was married to a somebody, she had to be a nobody. She got herself a job as a teacher, took the chair of the overseas development charity One World Action, among other organisations, and managed to fulfil her responsibilities to them without neglecting her role as a mother to her children. Just like the other two wives, she was there for them when they needed her and she worried about them every bit as much. 'Of course I worried,' she says. 'I still worry now that they are teenagers. It is not easy being a teenager at the best of times, it's infinitely more complicated when your father is leader of a political party.' She was concerned about the wearing day-to-day problems which she knew that they had to face, such as the people around them who, perhaps not knowing who they were, would suddenly exclaim that they thought Kinnock – they would always use the surname – was a bloody fool or worse. Stephen and Rachel must have got used to all that, she supposes, because they never came to her complaining. They had never said, not once, that they wished their father did a different job. She says that she admired them for that.

With the bulk of the newspapers in Britain so fervently hostile to the Labour Party, Mrs Kinnock had inevitably had to come to terms with criticism of a kind which Norma and Mrs Ashdown, at the outset of the campaign, could not have imagined even in their worst nightmares. Since her husband became the party leader in 1983, the press etched on to the minds of large sections of the electorate a stark picture of Glenys Kinnock as a shrill, opinionated old harridan who mercilessly bossed her husband around, and cynically used her position to propagate her own pet causes. They called her 'Glenys the Menace', 'Greenham Glenys', even 'the Red in Neil's bed'. Mrs Kinnock jokingly called it 'the Lady Macbeth number' and accepted the inevitability of the attacks, and handled them, some of her fiercest critics now quietly concede, with considerable dignity and good humour. She realised early on, she says, that the only way to survive the barrage was never to let on that she was hurting – and sue if it was actionable.

Mrs Kinnock knew very well that Norma was going to have an easier time of it during the campaign than herself simply because she had had the good fortune to have married a man who joined the party which had the approval of the overwhelming majority of the national newspapers, but she felt no envy or bitterness about that. In fact, she too says that she had a high regard for Norma: 'I genuinely think that she is a very nice person. I like her a lot. Reporters have been trying for ages to get me to say something nasty about her. Not one of them has succeeded.'

In the run-up to the campaign – that long, phoney war which waged for months until John finally named the date – the friendship between Mrs Kinnock and Norma was sorely tested. It was under greatest pressure when a story appeared on the front page of the *Sunday Telegraph* which claimed that the Labour Party's campaign managers had perceived Norma to be the Tories' Achilles' heel and had therefore decided to pit her against Mrs Kinnock, whom they considered an infinitely superior campaigner.

The story infuriated Mrs Kinnock when she saw it. 'I would never have wanted anything of that kind to have taken place – it simply wasn't the way I would have wished to have operated,' she insists. 'The idea of doing anything to hurt Norma would have disgusted me.' Labour's campaign manager Jack Cunningham immediately wrote to Chris Patten, his opposite number at Conservative Central Office, to make it clear that the story was wholly without foundation. Cunningham says: 'Mrs Major never figured in any of our discussions about the campaign. Had anyone suggested that we should have targeted her, I can assure you that I would personally have vetoed it. To this day, it remains a complete mystery to me how it ever arose.'

As it happened, it arose at an off-the-record briefing to Sunday newspaper lobby journalists given by Labour's press spokesman, Dave Hill. 'I was asked how Mrs Kinnock would be deployed in the campaign,' Hill says. 'I replied that we considered her a great asset and would be using her as much as possible. Then I added that I imagined Mrs Kinnock would be enjoying herself rather more during the campaign than Mrs Major. No more questions were asked and we moved on to other subjects.'

Self-interest dictates that lobby journalists attending these sort of briefings should stick together when the official that they have spoken to disputes what he has been quoted as saying, but on this occasion it was impossible to find anyone who attended it who was prepared to say that he had actually heard Hill categorically state that Labour was going to target Norma. One of them said feebly that the most he had done was to have implied it. Yet, to rub salt into the wound for the Labour Party, a number of newspaper columnists took up the story, saying that it showed just how low the party was prepared to sink to win the election if its managers were willing to attack a housewife who had the temerity not to behave like a politician.

As specious as the original story was, it turned out to be an extraordinarily lucky break for Norma. It had the effect of making the vaguest murmur of criticism about her among her husband's political opponents out of the question from that point onwards. Better still, it succeeded in bringing out a fighting spirit in the woman herself. Peter Brown, John's agent, was at Finings on the morning when the papers arrived and she saw the story for the first time. 'She was like a bat out of hell when she saw it,' he says. 'She shouted, "They are bloody well not going to get me." I think up until that point she had been apprehensive about the campaign, but for her that story was the turning point.'

As the campaign proper got under way, it soon became clear that, even if she had really wanted to, Norma was not going to be allowed to come out fighting. On the morning the election was called, an ambitious twenty-eight-year-old press officer from Conservative Central Office, Vanessa Ford, turned up at Finings at nine o'clock and attached herself, limpet-like, to Norma, where she was to remain for the duration of the campaign. Her job – though she defined it more tactfully – was principally to stop her charge talking to anyone that the party considered inappropriate, which seemed, such was their faith in her abilities, to be just about everybody.

Among Norma's friends there was dismay that Central Office felt it necessary to assign her a 'minder'. In political terms, it was the equivalent to being ordered to wear water-wings. Olive Baddeley says that it was humiliating because it gave the impression that she could not cope on her own. Norma was not a woman who would be happy being directed and manipulated. It so happened, Mrs Baddeley points out, that Norma had got through quite a few elections standing perfectly well on her own two feet long before her minder had even left school.

Mrs Kinnock and Mrs Ashdown, old hands at the game, would have raised merry hell if either of their parties had tried imposing a Vanessa Ford on them. They had nothing personal against the young woman herself; it was what she represented that they found so repellent: the all-encompassing power and arrogance of modern party managers. As everyone knew very well, Ms Ford was there not to look after Norma's interests, but the interests of the party. Her very presence at Mrs Major's side showed that Central Office regarded her as little more than a liability during the campaign. 'I felt for Norma when I saw her there with that woman,' says Mrs Ashdown. 'It must have been horrible for her.'

Central Office even had ideas about roping in the Majors' children. They expended much effort in trying to persuade Elizabeth and James to campaign with their parents for a day. Elizabeth made her opposition to the idea perfectly clear. Unknown to her, Central Office then invited journalists to a charity concert in which she was appearing in Huntingdon, hinting that she would be prepared to give them an interview after it was over. When she was told that a photographer was outside she told the organiser not to let him in. Asked for a few words, she almost growled her refusal.

Mrs Kinnock says that it is always necessary to be firm with party managers. Show them toughness and they will respect it, show the merest hint of weakness and they will take advantage. She made it painstakingly clear from the moment that her husband was elected leader that she would not take kindly to anyone trying to manipulate her. Peter Mandelson, the Svengali behind Labour's new look, would raise his eyebrows from time to time, such as the occasion when she agreed to appear on the *Dame Edna Everage Show*, but, she says, he always knew that he finally had to leave such decisions to her.

Of all the players in the campaign, Norma was the only one allotted what was almost exclusively a non-speaking part. It pleased the photographers, if not the writers. They snapped her making a rare visit to church with her husband on Mothering Sunday (the Majors are not, their friends say, especially religious), trying to fly a kite with the comedian Roy Hudd on an unusually still day for the Spinal Research Trust, and collecting a bright red Peugeot to raffle for the Breakthrough Breast Cancer Appeal in London (a charity she took a particular interest in after June Bronhill developed the disease).

None of the pictures that they took of Norma was especially flattering. She was not as photogenic as Mrs Kinnock, a natural in front of the cameras with a dazzling smile, or Mrs Ashdown, who, despite calling herself 'a scruffy cow', always came across marvellously, especially in moody Jane Bown-style close-ups. Norma's nerves and the evident strain of the campaign invariably had her breaking the most rudimentary rules of working with photographers and cameramen: she blinked, hunched herself up, never seemed to know what to do with her hands, and her smiles looked painfully forced. This was ironic because great attention seemed to have been paid to getting Norma's 'look' right for the cameras. Mrs Ashdown was not alone in thinking that she looked horribly like a woman who had been 'done over' by the party's image-makers – the hair, the clothes, the make-up, all had that particular Stepford Wife sheen about them. The hair and the make-up, Norma had admitted, had been adjusted by outsiders, but she was indignant at the suggestion, often made during the campaign, that she would need help dressing herself. Her all-British wardrobe of Windsmoor (for day wear) and Frank Usher (evenings) was, she insisted, entirely her own selection. That she so often wore red and yellow – the colours of Labour and the Liberal Democrats respectively – suggests that she was telling the truth. Norma was no clothes-horse, however. When she was hosting a reception to launch London Fashion Week, the *Guardian*'s Andrew Rawnsley noted that the main sport was playing Norma off against Mrs Thatcher, the hostess of previous years. 'Norma doesn't *glow* in the way that Margaret did,' he overheard one American buyer saying. 'She looks like she could make an incredible cup of tea . . . and that's about it.'

On several occasions Norma even had to suffer the indignity of being upstaged by her own minder. Miss Ford, who happened to be a stunningly attractive woman, had an unfortunate habit of wearing the same colours as her charge, and, worse, found that at a number of press conferences a lot of the photographers were more interested in taking pictures of her. 'I hate it, I'll lose my job,' she groaned, but still took the opportunity to hand out a pretentious business card listing her full qualifications: BA (Hons) Dip CAM MIPR. The man from the *Daily Mirror*, while not quite sure what all that meant, thought she brightened up the campaign enormously, and wrote: 'She outshines nerdy Norma every time.'

As amusing as it all might have appeared to some, Ms Ford was seen by Central Office to be playing a vitally important role. They appeared terrified at the prospect of somebody just wandering up and having an unscheduled word with Norma. At all costs, she was to ensure that Norma was seen and not heard. The BBC political correspondent Nicholas Jones saw Norma sitting alone in one of the press seats at the Queen Elizabeth II conference centre in London when the party launched its manifesto. 'I overheard party workers anxiously saying that they must make sure journalists did not get too close to Mrs Major because we might ask questions and she might find this unsettling,' he says. The journalists travelling with the Majors during the campaign were left in no doubt that it was against the rules to solicit even the quickest quote from Norma without prior permission. After John Sweeney, a highly-respected reporter from the *Observer*, had his accreditation summarily withdrawn in somewhat mysterious circumstances, most of the journalists reluctantly felt it best to play it by the rules.

A small handful of newspaper interviews were still unavoidable for Norma, but all were with journalists carefully selected and approved by Central Office, and the ubiquitous Ms Ford sat in on all of them. Her presence seemed to bring out the best in Norma's interrogators. None of them thought to raise, for instance, the politically sensitive matter of Norma's education, even after one of her old classmates from Peckham School for Girls, latterly Peckham Comprehensive, had raised the matter in the *Guardian* letters page: 'The Conservative Party has kept

quiet about Mrs Major's educational origins while trumpeting
forth her husband's experiences as a grammar school drop-out,'
she had written. 'No doubt it would not suit the party's fixed
ideas on education to recognise the considerable debt owed by
Norma to her former school, both in terms of career and of
character.'

Funnily enough, the very same journalists who had been
straining not to upset Norma were then apparently turning up on
Mrs Kinnock's doorstep and showing the other side of their
personalities. 'They always kept the heavy political questions for
me – all the difficult ones about religion and South Africa,' says
Mrs Kinnock. 'I hardly ever got hair and make-up. Oh, that they
would have permitted me to spend half an hour talking about
hair and make-up.' Every word that Mrs Kinnock came out with
was carefully analysed and evaluated by the journalists, who
were eager to find something that could embarrass her husband
or have been turned into a joke against him. (Had Mrs Kinnock –
and not Norma – spoken in an election-time interview about her
nightmare of waking up and finding a snake in her bed, there
would have been few newspapers who wouldn't have suggested a
name for it!)

Central Office had a very particular idea of how they wanted
to present the Majors to the electorate. They saw that trying to
invest either of them with any glamour would be a hopeless task:
John, with his Steve Martin hairstyle, and coat-hanger lips, was
no Jack Kennedy, and Norma, for that matter, was no Jackie. So
they concentrated their efforts instead in making a virtue of their
ordinariness. John was honest John, 'pug ugly' – his own phrase
– but a man of the people who enjoyed fry-ups at motorway
service stations, liked to watch cricket on the TV at weekends,
and put in a fair day's work for a fair day's pay. As for the
woman he married, they wanted to cast her as a kind of
overgrown girl guide, a well-intentioned 'jolly hockey sticks'
type in the perennially popular Joyce Grenfell mould.

Eve Pollard, the editor of the *Sunday Express*, gave the party a God-given opportunity to present Norma to the public when she invited her to write an election diary for the paper. The ghost-writer that the paper had somewhat presumptuously assigned Norma (the veteran woman's page journalist Joyce Hopkirk) was informed that her services would not be required and the first instalment of Mrs Major's Diary was duly faxed to the paper to length and (just) ahead of deadline from the Major campaign bus. Ms Pollard, who had paid Mencap a substantial sum for the privilege of using Norma's byline, read it with a distinct lack of enthusiasm on her face. Ordinariness, she discovered, did not translate as good copy.

Among the more interesting snippets which Norma chose to share with the readers was the fact that her washing-machine had gone on the blink; a button had fallen off her jacket (calamity had however been averted because, good girl guide that she was, she'd had a needle and cotton handy); on a journey to Doncaster she had taken a jar of Bovril with her and had made herself a hot drink from it; and, to her great excitement, she had got to see Bill Roache, the star of her favourite TV series, *Coronation Street*. Had the piece appeared in *Private Eye* as a spoof nobody would have thought anything of it. In the following weeks, Mrs Major's Diary had a considerably smaller slot in the paper due to what Ms Hopkirk diplomatically refers to as 'pressures of space'.

Later instalments included an occasional heavy-handed swipe at the Labour Party (she noted once that their supporters were 'making a terrible din and were not very photogenic . . . I wonder if they will bother to vote!') but, reading between the lines, the campaign was not something that she had got terribly worked up about. At Accrington, she said that she got waylaid and missed John unveiling a plaque. On another night, at the height of the campaign, she disclosed that she was in bed by ten o'clock; she missed no opportunity during the campaign to touch base at Huntingdon; she didn't watch her husband's big interview with Sir Robin Day; and she put off a campaign appointment because she considered it less important than getting the washing machine fixed at Finings.

The cheery folksiness of Norma's diary belied her real mood during the campaign. To the reporters who saw her on a daily basis it was clear that she was not enjoying herself. It was a tense, fraught time, not only for her but for just about everybody involved in it. Harvey Thomas, who left Central Office after a contretemps with its abrasive communications director, Shaun Woodward, says he formed the opinion that the campaign was not being professionally run and that there was no overall strategy. Sir Peregrine Worsthorne, the *Sunday Telegraph* columnist, wrote that the people in charge of it didn't seem quite human. Rumours abounded of rows on the campaign bus and Norma herself was said to have been angry with Woodward for allowing her so little freedom. Woodward pointedly refuses to talk about how he deployed Norma during the campaign, as did her minder, Vanessa Ford, who says darkly that she had orders 'from above' not to say anything.

After one day's campaigning, Norma spoke of her delight at being able to escape from her husband's entourage for a few precious moments to talk to some ordinary people. The party officials and the accredited members of the press who accompanied her were not, she had belatedly realised, ordinary people. When an official on the bus asked her if she cared to place a bet on Party Politics for the Grand National, she snapped back: 'Certainly not. I'm sick of party politics.'

She was also getting sick of the journalists. One in particular, Carina Trimingham, a doggedly persistent reporter for Sky TV News, annoyed her so much when she asked John why his campaign was 'such a shambles' that she took her aside afterwards to complain. 'She took it all very, very personally, which was something I found rather surprising in the wife of a politician at John's level,' says Ms Trimingham. 'She considered such questions negative and downright rude. She didn't seem to think that reporters should ask her husband things which might upset him.' She recalls that, after that incident, whenever she asked the Prime Minister anything awkward, Norma would be standing there beside him tut-tutting and shaking her head disapprovingly, and she would know that she was going to get a ticking-off afterwards.

Some reporters on the campaign bus claim that there was *froideur* between Norma and her husband and say that they seemed to be keeping themselves to themselves, seldom, if ever, talking. 'Normy, come on, you're holding us up,' John said to her at one campaign stop, as she was talking to some local party workers. 'That makes a change, doesn't it – I'm always the one waiting for *you*,' she replied. At a campaign stop in Melton Mowbray, one reporter says he couldn't help noticing Norma jokingly patting the handsome local MP, Alan Duncan, on the bottom. John's soap-box orations in city centres meant that Norma was invariably pressed up close to her husband, often having no alternative but to stare, dejectedly, into his crotch. Her worst moment in the campaign came at Bolton when John addressed his most hostile audience. When it looked, at one point, as if the police were going to be overwhelmed by a crowd of almost a thousand protesters, several reporters heard her crying in terror: 'Get me out of here, John.' As it happened, she did get out, unscathed, and afterwards took the curious step of asking a TV company to provide her with a video of the event so that she could review her ordeal at her leisure.

Norma's and Mrs Kinnock's problems during the campaign pale into insignificance when put beside those of Mrs Ashdown. Having gone into it so unsuspectingly, she found her world suddenly thrown into turmoil after the newspapers learnt of her husband's brief affair with a secretary six years previously. Overnight her private life became a national spectacle. The *Sun*, mustering all its customary good taste and sensitivity, declared in a banner headline 'It's Paddy Pants Down'. When Mrs Ashdown ventured out she was assailed by journalists. 'Did you know that your husband has just admitted to the affair?' one of them shouted at her. 'Has he? Well, well, well,' she replied. Later she came out and asked the man and his colleagues if they would care for a cup of tea. It was a rare sight during the election campaign: an example of grace under pressure. (But it was not an original idea: the 'fragrant' Mary Archer had famously brought out cups of tea for journalists after the libellous allegations of her husband's fling with a prostitute.)

In a TV interview, Norma said that she felt 'desperately sorry' for Mrs Ashdown, and Mrs Kinnock made similar public pronouncements, but neither of them thought to contact her privately. Mrs Ashdown understood. 'In this business,' she says, 'it is sometimes difficult to express concern for people without even that being misinterpreted as political point-scoring.'

The experience, interestingly, did not make Mrs Ashdown come round to the other wives' view that laws should be introduced to curb the press, and she says that, taking everything into account, she believes that she was actually treated fairly by the press – no better or no worse than the others. As to whether she could see a rationale to it all, she says: 'The judgement of newspaper editors becomes warped and distorted at election times and stories which would usually hardly warrant any space at all end up on the front pages for days and days. My husband's affair was just another example – it had no relevance to the campaign, and, indeed, it had no effect on it. The stories achieved absolutely nothing besides causing my husband, myself and my children a lot of pain. Looking back on it now, I wonder what on earth was the point.'

Like so many other aspects of the campaign, it was, Mrs Ashdown feels, so very American. 'We've got to the stage now that we're putting everyone who goes into politics under the microscope and picking over every misdemeanour, just as they do on the other side of the Atlantic. If we'd had this in the past, we'd have been deprived of so many great leaders, including Churchill, who it was, I think, who said that men of genius possess in general shortcomings commensurate with their abilities. The fact is people who have never done anything wrong in their lives tend to be incredibly bland and haven't the spirit and passion which a leader needs. Or they are just hypocrites who haven't broken the cardinal rule about being found out.'

The political commentator Ed Pearce, a veteran of many campaigns, said '92 was the fiercest ever fought. For Norma it certainly wasn't easy. On one of the last campaign stops, John's bar-stool meeting at Tooting, she ran into her old friend Clive Jones. 'How's it going?' he asked. Norma threw her arms around him and whispered into his ear: 'You know, Clive, I'll just be glad when it's over.'

In their assessments of how the three wives fared during the campaign, the party professionals were predictably partisan. Harvey Thomas, for the Conservatives, says: 'Norma came across as intelligent, calm and loyal. She might have angered the feminists by saying that she was happy simply to be a good wife and mother, but the feminists are a minority, so that didn't hurt in political terms. Norma was very good for John because people must have thought he must be a good, decent man to have the love of such a fine woman. As for Mrs Kinnock, I felt that she was a liability. The problem was that her husband had done U-turns on so many issues, such as unilateral disarmament, which she still believed in. Seeing Mrs Kinnock at his side, one was just made more aware than ever of his lack of conviction. I have a great respect for Mrs Ashdown, but I think that her calm, dignified response to her husband's infidelity cost him dear in political terms. People wondered how he could have done such a thing to a woman with her qualities. Funnily enough, had he been seen to have been married to some loud-mouthed old harpy, it might have been more understandable.'

The Labour Party's Dave Hill says that he was delighted with the way that Mrs Kinnock had come across during the campaign.

'The public liked her. They always did. They saw through the rubbish that was printed about her in the papers. Of course she had her own views, but people respected her for that. She came across as a real person, just as Mrs Ashdown did, but, with Mrs Major, the electorate were never really allowed to know what she was thinking.'

That was a view shared by the Liberal Democrats' Des Wilson. 'To me, Norma never looked as if she was enjoying herself during the campaign. She reminded me of Pat Nixon, and, to be honest, I felt rather sorry for her.' He says that he personally had a high regard for Mrs Kinnock as a campaigner and believed that she had done much in her own right to update the Labour Party's image. As for his own leader's wife, he says: 'I just left Jane to it and she got along marvellously, as she always does. Obviously it wasn't an easy campaign for her, but I would defy anyone to find fault with anything that she did or said.'

It was finally all over for the wives on 9 April, Election Day. John called it his gift to Norma because it happened to be the twenty-second anniversary of the day that he had first set eyes upon her. The Ashdowns, the Kinnocks and the Majors all dealt with the trauma of that agonisingly long day in their own ways.

'I felt a terrible feeling of uncertainty,' says Mrs Ashdown. 'It was like walking around on a battlefield after the last shot had been fired and not knowing who had won because the smoke still hadn't cleared.'

Mrs Kinnock admits that she was consciously making herself say all the right things, but, inside, she didn't feel right about the way it was going. The polls had got her hopes up, but, somehow, she just couldn't take the leap of faith that was required for her to see herself in No. 10 with Neil. 'In the final few days of the campaign, I had seen something different in the way that people were looking at me; I'd heard something different in their voices,' she says. 'I had this almost palpable feeling that they were turning away from us.'

Over a cup of tea, she said to Neil: 'We'll have such a party if we win.'

He smiled at her and replied: 'We'll have an even bigger party if we lose.' Then he said: 'You don't think we are going to win, do you?'

'No, I don't,' she replied.

The Majors had a quiet day at Finings. A reporter had telephoned early in the morning and got James, who was still in his dressing-gown, and asked him what his plans were for the day. 'I imagine I'll just mooch around the house,' he replied impatiently. 'I'm a teenager – what sort of things do you expect me to do?'

The whole family sat down together for lunch with Sue Winn and Lord Archer, a near neighbour at Grantchester, joining them. The opinion polls made it a subdued affair. Archer asked John if he worried about the effect a full term at No. 10 might have on his family. John replied: 'If I thought this was really going to upset Norma and the children – if I thought it was going to ruin our family life – then I would rather lose the election.' The conversation then turned to what John would do if he did lose the election – Archer hastily adding the rider that that was of course highly unlikely. There was an uncomfortable silence. Norma finally made a joke of it: 'If we do lose, I just hope that they won't make John leave by the back door.' James, ever the practical one, chipped in jauntily: 'For one thing, we'll have 3,000 fewer cards to send out this Christmas.' John was more serious: 'You must understand that it isn't the be-all and the end-all, for goodness' sake. Good heavens, there are plenty of other things I could do.'

That night, when it became clear that John had won the election, Norma went down to London with him along with James and Elizabeth, Norma was hugged warmly by her husband's innumerable supporters, including Margaret Thatcher.

Mrs Ashdown watched the results unfold in silence. 'It was knowing the personal circumstances of a lot of the candidates who lost their seats that made it so awful,' she says. 'When I heard Michael Carr had lost, I thought of his wife and seven children and I wondered what on earth he was going to do. Then there was Jackie Ballard, who had given up her job and moved house to fight her seat and I knew that she had thought she had a good chance of winning.'

Just before midnight, when they learned that the Tories had held the marginal seat of Basildon, Mrs Kinnock saw the look on her husband's face as he realised it was all over. He turned round to her and said wearily: 'That's it, love, that's it.' Dressed in an incongruously cheerful pink suit, she went with him to the Town Hall in his constituency in Islwyn, and appeared surprised when he began his speech by paying a warm, personal tribute to her: 'In this campaign she has been the target of such spite that it disgraces those who offer it. And she bears it with a dignity that makes me proud of her as well as love her very dearly.'

Mrs Kinnock says: 'I suppose it was typical of my husband, really, in what must have been the single most painful moment of his life, to have worried about what *I* was feeling.'

When she arrived with him at the Labour Party headquarters in Walworth Road at 5.30 on the cold, dank morning of 10 April, she listened, her face a picture of despair, as he finally laid the dream to rest and conceded defeat. 'I wanted to cry,' she admits. 'I came very close to it, but somehow I managed to hold on.' The tears welled up in her eyes, but they never burst through. It was when Neil said he didn't feel sorry for himself because he was so fortunate in his personal life that she seemed closest to losing her composure. As he turned to go, several journalists shouted at her husband: 'Goodbye, loser.'

A few hours later John made his victory speech outside No. 10 with Norma there beside him, and, when he saw her inadvertently wandering over to where the reporters were, he pulled her back and guided her inside.

Mrs Ashdown stayed at home in Yeovil, getting on with the housework. She says: 'The place was a tip. I couldn't remember when I'd last hoovered. The phone kept ringing – so many people wanted to say how sorry they were – and, on the TV set in the corner of the room, I saw John and Norma Major waving to the crowds and smiling. I felt animosity towards the electorate, but not towards them. Actually I remember feeling quite sorry for Norma. I thought at least 90 per cent of her life from that point on was not going to be her own.'

Mrs Ashdown did her best to build up Paddy ('That's the job of the politician's wife after another bloody defeat,' she says) and when they first spoke, after the final result was known, she told him: 'Never mind, darling, it doesn't matter.' Secretly – she never told him this – she wanted to go into her garden and shout as loudly as she could, to anyone who would listen: 'How could you be so STUPID?'

The curtains were drawn, the blinds pulled down and the telephone was off the hook at the Kinnocks' home in Ealing. Mrs Kinnock had a barbecue planned for the evening which she decided that it would be best to go ahead with. Relatives, a few old friends, nothing special – it was to have been a celebration. Rachel and Stephen were, like her, both despondent, but Neil was, as ever, the perfect host, saying all the right things, making jokes, even laughing. Mrs Kinnock slipped out, and, where no one could see her, she finally allowed herself to cry.

It bothered Mrs Kinnock that her husband held it all in. If he could only let it all out, the effect would have been cathartic, but, no, he said, he felt it would be self-indulgent. The house was full of letters of commiseration and flowers from well-wishers, almost as if someone had died, which was quite appropriate actually because Mrs Kinnock says there was a sense of be-reavement in the household. Somebody asked her if she would have been prepared to have gone through everything she had if she had known how it was going to end. 'Yes,' she said, without hesitation.

A reporter asked Norma if she could have coped if John had lost. John had only been in No. 10 for sixteen months, she had replied, so, no, it wouldn't have been difficult to have gone back to a normal life. The family had not yet lost touch with what it had had before. She would have been perfectly happy, she said.

As it was, Norma returned to Finings, the reluctant victor in the Battle of the First Ladies. Her immediate priorities: 'to do the shopping, washing and ironing – all the naff things that need to be done.' The day after the election, Baroness Blatch saw her in Woolworth's with her mother. 'What are you two doing?' she inquired. 'We're buying Easter eggs for the staff at Chequers,' Norma replied.

CHAPTER 7

Being There

JOHN AND NORMA are great fans of Peter Sellers and it so happens that their favourite film is the actor's last, *Being There*. It is the story of Chance the Gardener, a dull, simple soul, overlooked by all those around him, who, by a bizarre trick of fate, one day finds himself at the centre of the political arena. It is a very good film, the sort just about anybody would enjoy, but it is intriguing that the Majors should like it so much. Although neither of them could be called simple, they both share some of the central character's innocent, unworldly quality.

The Majors' friends in politics know that they *are* different. John's agent Peter Brown, a man with years of experience in the Conservative Party, says that he had never encountered people like them before in his life. 'I suppose,' he says thoughtfully, 'that it's their ordinariness which sets them apart.'

There are countless stories of how John and Norma have themselves been struck by the incongruity of 'people like them' occupying such elevated positions in public life. In the past, Tory Prime Ministers and their wives often appeared to regard No. 10 as theirs by God-given right, Chequers as just another country home to attend to, and other world statesmen merely as excitable foreigners. Nobody could ever have imagined Lady Macmillan

149

talking about her excitement at meeting somebody like Frank Sinatra or an actor from *Coronation Street* or, for that matter, 'SuperMac' beginning his first cabinet with the phrase: 'Who'd have thought it?' Through everything that has happened, the Majors have somehow managed to stay the same.

Baroness Blatch tells one of those inconsequential little stories about the Majors which speaks reams about them. She was sitting in the kitchen at Finings chatting to them both when John said something about how they had just got back from the Great Wall of China, and, as he mentioned it, he caught Norma's eye and the two of them started giggling. 'They both seemed to be thinking "Imagine *us* being on the Great Wall of China."' Blatch was very struck by that. 'Given who they are and the positions that they occupy, I must say that I found it rather charming,' she says. 'A lot of people might see in that sort of behaviour something to mock or be patronising about, but I think it's something we should cherish. With John and Norma, it really is a case of what you see is what you get.'

John's former agent Andrew Thomson remembers that when the Majors first arrived in Huntingdon, they used to delight in finding a constituent who had come, like them, from Lambeth. They had a great nostalgia for the place where they had begun their married life and seemed suddenly to come alive when they started talking about it. In one sense, they have never left Lambeth. Their values and their attitudes have remained the same, only the scale has changed: now they have tetchy François and Danielle living across the road, struggling Boris and Naina always coming over for butter, and, in the big house where their old friends George and Barbara used to live, there's that new couple, Bill and Hillary.

To the distinguished psychologist and writer Dr Dorothy Rowe, the Majors' tendency to separate themselves from their roles – this feeling of 'fancy us doing something like this, rubbing shoulders with all these people who are so much more important than we are' – betrays a deep-rooted sense of insecurity. The Americans call it the 'imposter syndrome': a pop term describing the serious problem, increasingly prevalent of people playing roles throughout their lives to disguise the fact that they have little or no sense of their own identity or worth.

Dr Rowe sees much in both John's and Norma's backgrounds which points to theirs being classic cases. During their formative years, neither had the full attention of two loving parents from whose praise and criticism they could have derived a proper sense of themselves and their own strengths and weaknesses. Norma spent those years in boarding-schools being supervised only by a succession of teachers. John's earliest recollections of his father were as an old and frail man whose ill health took up almost all his mother's time. John was left, as Norma was, to fend for himself – desperately self-conscious and lacking in confidence, but as determined as she was to improve his station in life, which would bring with it, he hoped, the emotional stability he must have known, deep down, that he was missing.

In their adult lives, Dr Rowe sees the syndrome manifesting itself in myriad ways in both their characters. John lived his life through a political party; Norma at first through opera stars, and then through her role as a mother. Neither of them wanted to change the world – the most frequently voiced criticism of John is that he hasn't got a 'vision' of his own – and, according to people who have known them through the years, neither appeared to have changed much themselves. Norma admitted that she was slow to mature, worried that people might not think her bright enough, and said, only half in jest, that she felt that she had never grown up. When he became Prime Minister, John complained, as he had complained when he was a teenager in his first job in the City, that he felt people were looking down their noses at him. Even after he achieved the highest office in the land, he still, unbelievably, feels inferior.

Both John and Norma have been prone to severe mood swings, and there are the occasional outbursts of temper within the privacy of their own home, invariably directed at each other or the children because they are the only ones unlucky enough to be around. Dr Rowe says that this too is consistent with imposter syndrome: by putting on an act so much of the time they necessarily have to bottle up their emotions, which periodically explode when the pressure becomes too intense. Alternatively, it could affect their health, as it did Norma's, when she said, after John became Foreign Secretary, that she felt 'physically sick' and started losing weight. John himself reportedly had an energy-sapping illness at the time of the Bermuda Summit in 1991.

There is no stigma attached to this 'imposter syndrome'. In many ways, it is an endearing trait and certainly eminently more attractive than the insufferable arrogance and self-obsession of John Major's predecessor. It becomes a problem only when things don't go according to plan. Having given themselves their roles and established their pattern of life, Dr Rowe says that they will always find it difficult to adjust to change, which explains why John often appears to be at a loss when revisions in government policy are forced upon him (such as the withdrawal from the ERM), and why Norma balked when a whole new series of duties suddenly landed on her plate when John became Foreign Secretary and later Prime Minister. The slightest criticism wounds them deeply because, still having no sense of their own identity, they are unable to laugh it off or treat it with appropriate contempt. So it was that John and Norma made a joint decision to issue writs against two low-circulation publications after they ran unsubstantiated stories linking John to Clare Latimer, a professional caterer, even though many observers believed the action belittled the office of the Prime Minister. The trouble is that the only sense of identity that John and Norma have comes from what other people say about them.

Dr Rowe also points to the Majors' curious lack of spontaneity in public. With Jane and Paddy Ashdown, Neil and Glenys Kinnock and subsequently John Smith, it has always been clear, even when they are on television, whether they are happy or unhappy. With John and Norma, it is difficult to make the distinction. There are hardly any known instances of either of them losing their temper or shouting in public, or, by the same token, showing signs of being obviously joyous, or getting silly, or even drunk – the masks are never allowed to slip. As Norma says: 'I suppose I have always worked as opposed to played.'

But for all that, the Majors' friends obviously have a very deep and enduring affection for them. There is something reassuring about a couple who never seem to change, and it is difficult, after all, not to like people whose only objective in life is to be liked – the most obvious characteristic of imposter syndrome.

Their closest friends, like them, old-fashioned people with old-fashioned views, scoff at the suggestion that there could possibly be any highfalutin' psychological term which could apply to the Majors. John and Norma themselves were predictably distressed when the phrase was first used in relation to them in a précis of this book which appeared in the publisher's catalogue. The problem with John and Norma is that a fundamental element of the roles that they have assigned themselves – good working-class British stock modelled straight from a 1950s Jack Warner film – is to make the best of things and muddle through, no matter what. They would be the last people in the world to admit that there might be a problem.

It is vitally important to John and Norma, perhaps more important than it has been to any other couple who have made it into No. 10, that they are perceived to be successful. They know that that is the only way to silence the snobs, the intellectuals and indeed the psychologists who have all thought, for their different reasons, that they might be unequal to the challenge. On present reckoning, however, the final chapter in the life of the Majors does not look as if it is going to end happily. The fate that is befalling John is almost the exact opposite of what happened to Chance the Gardener in *Being There*. Instead of being a simple man who came to be regarded as a man who had the makings of a great national leader, John is, all too often, thought of as quite the reverse. Whether the Establishment is giving him a fair crack of the whip is debatable, but the Classless Man is beginning to be seen to be a failure.

In the winter following the General Election, one poll revealed that John was the most unpopular Prime Minister that the country had seen since records began. The enduring image of him during those months was painted by anomymous 'friends' quoted in newspaper articles, including in *The Times* which spoke of him spending his evenings sitting alone in his private quarters at No. 10, drinking cans of beer and picking at Chinese take-aways as *News at Ten* spelt out the latest on the economy, the pit closures, Maastricht and the arms to Iraq affair. Lord Archer, the hapless jester to the court of John Major in its darkest hour, desperately tried to cheer his leader up by getting his friends to phone him in relays.

The Times article even claimed that he dyed his hair – *grey*, presumably – something that he was able to joke about when his sister Pat Dessoy telephoned. 'I can't talk to you now,' he said. 'I'm too busy dying my hair.' John could laugh too when his brother Terry rang, and, alluding to a paragraph which said that John was losing weight, Terry started the conversation by saying, 'Hello, Porky.' But for all the good humour, Mrs Dessoy says that her brother was deeply disturbed by the press coverage he was getting. He is, as she says, a man given to dwelling on such things.

Those days were no easier for Norma. The sight of Tory MPs laying into her own husband severely shook her faith in the Conservative Party. She speculated with Dulcie Atkins on how a 'new breed' of Tory MPs had entered Parliament who couldn't really care less about John because they knew that in ten years' time, when they had made it on to the front benches, he would be yesterday's man. 'But what they don't seem to understand is that that's the *Prime Minister* they are talking about,' Norma said. 'There's no respect there any more.' She told Nesta Wyn Ellis that she felt people had started 'slacking' and become 'Bolshie' during John's premiership because he didn't 'crack the whip' as Mrs Thatcher had. A loyal *Daily Mail* reader, Norma was shaken when that newspaper saw fit to make serious criticisms of her husband. Unlike her patrician predecessor Lady Home, so unperturbed by these little matters of *lèse-majesté* that she once acquired a newspaper billboard bearing the words 'Home – A Disaster' as an amusing souvenir, Norma took it all very much to heart. 'It depresses her terribly when people say awful things about John,' says Mrs Atkins. 'She knows very well the power of words, and so, no, she can't just shrug it off.'

Norma herself was not immune to press criticism during that long, hard winter. It did not, of course, go unnoticed that the one person John might most obviously turn to for succour, his wife, was pressing on with her routine at Finings, apparently oblivious to what was happening in London. On the front page of *Private Eye* there was a picture of Norma walking away from her husband, who was crying out for her not to desert him as well as everyone else.

Norma had her own reasons for staying on at Finings, then as now. She knows very well that politicians need to surround themselves with people who bolster their confidence. She found it hard enough to cope with the idea of John as the Foreign Secretary, and later said that she found it surreal to hear MPs in the Commons referring to him as the Chancellor. The thought of him being the Prime Minister must therefore be even harder for her to deal with.

There is another, perhaps more fundamental, reason. It is likely that she feels she no longer knows her husband well enough to help him. Since he became an MP in 1979, she has only ever seen him at weekends, if that, and, inevitably, the two of them have grown apart. In a remarkably frank admission, Norma said that John had long since ceased to be at the centre of her life. She employed the most sterile of phrases – 'very equitable' – to describe her relationship with her husband. For his part, John noted, with typical understatement, that politics is a tough trade for married people.

There is a poignant story of how a school in Huntingdon had written to Norma asking for a photograph of herself with her husband for them to raffle. She had had to send them two separate photographs, explaining plaintively that things had been moving so quickly in their lives that it hadn't been possible to organise a joint one. For a lot of people who knew John and Norma well, the two photographs seemed symbolic.

The state of their marriage has been a talking point in Westminster for some years, and there have been rumours, dating from around the time when John was appointed Foreign Secretary, that Norma actually wanted a divorce. Asked directly whether there is any truth in this, a number of the Majors' friends become flustered and evasive, some indicating it is a subject that they aren't prepared to answer questions about, or saying that they simply don't know. Often it is the slips they make which seem the most telling. Baroness Blatch, talking about the period when John was in the Foreign Office, says: 'She had a marriage that was fairly safe – I mean *very* safe; one has to be careful how one phrases these things.' Ian Cameron Black came out with the curious phrase: 'It is a plausible scenario which I do not believe to have come about.' One friend says, on condition that it is not attributed to him, that there have indeed been crises in the marriage, but in the circumstances they would have had to have been a superhuman couple not to have had them. 'They're not as close as most couples are. Perhaps what they have isn't a marriage in the way that most people would understand it, but they've found a formula which suits their lifestyle, and that's what matters.'

Had John lost the election, it might have been very different. As Norma says: 'Maybe it's better to travel than to arrive.' Ironically, she seems almost jealous of Glenys Kinnock for having the time to set about rebuilding her family life after her husband's defeat. She saw a picture of her in the *Cambridge Evening News* standing proudly beside her handsome begowned son Stephen after he had graduated from Queen's, and read elsewhere that she was supervising the family's move to a new house, and was even managing to find the time to go to the theatre twice a week with Neil. 'I did feel, how nice for her, how pleasant,' Norma says wistfully. 'Wouldn't it be lovely to do that?'

That Norma is ultimately very unhappy with the way things have turned out in her life few of her friends doubt. Barbara Wallis says that she can count on the fingers of one hand the free weekends Norma now has with John in a year. Baroness Blatch speaks of the 'mournful' tone in Norma's voice when she complained to her that the civil servants in Whitehall saw more of her husband than she did. 'She would tell me "I can't even get five minutes with him on my own." She would say it in a way that suggested than the situation just could not go on, that it would *have* to stop,' she says.

The tragedy of course is that, so long as John drives himself with the same relentless determination, it cannot stop. Norma says: 'I would love just once to think that everything else didn't have to come before us. But the fact is I haven't had John to myself for a long time.' She might well have threatened divorce, but she is shrewd enough to know that it was never a serious option for her. Had she gone through with it, the media interest in her would have intensified a hundredfold, and outside the protective shield accorded to her as John's wife, she would have been vulnerable and exposed, with nowhere obvious to run. That is a prospect too horrific even to contemplate. And besides, all her friends insist that even if her husband isn't presently at the centre of her life and she hardly ever sees him, they do still love each other.

Over lunch at 'Le Caprice', one of the Majors' oldest friends, Robert Atkins, looked over at Princess Diana, a few months before the announcement of her separation, and said that he felt Norma's situation bore many parallels to hers. Both women were perceived to be living fairytale lives when privately, they were having to come to terms with intense personal pressures. 'It is easy to make cheap cracks about Norma's hair and her clothes,' he says. 'It takes a little more perception to appreciate what she is going through inside.' David Mellor blames the situation on the pressures that politicians are under today, running almost every hour of the day just to stand still. 'Under the present system, any man who reaches cabinet level can never have enough time for his wife,' he says. 'The fact is that if everyone in the cabinet did put their marriages first every time, the government would fall apart.'

John's agent Peter Brown says frankly that he doesn't believe that Norma can find real peace of mind until after John leaves No. 10. What keeps her going, he feels, is the fact that she knows it won't go on for ever. The day John walks out of No. 10 for the last time, she will finally be able to get on with her marriage in earnest. Then John will no longer have to worry about money, he will have realised his ambitions, he will no doubt still be in his fifties and, best of all, he will be able to offer her something he has never been able to offer her before: time. So it is not that her marriage has failed, it is just that, in many ways, it has been put on hold. As Norma says: 'It's fine. You do your own thing, you come together. There's no time to get bored with each other. I'm certainly not bored with him. It seems to work for us.'

Having had to make so many sacrifices in her life, it is understandable that Norma should have a somewhat rose-tinted view of the day that John leaves No. 10. She has a romantic dream of going up the Nile with him, something they have both wanted to do for some time, but have so far never had the chance. 'I think that she believes that she will be able to revert to her old life with John,' says Olive Baddeley. 'But I don't know whether she will really be able to.' Like so many Prime Ministers' wives before her, Norma seems not to appreciate that out of office John is likely to be a changed man. Like his predecessors, he will either be cast out by the electorate. betrayed by members of his own cabinet or put into a position in which he has no alternative but to resign. Whichever one of these fates awaits him, the effect upon him psychologically is likely to be profound. For the first time in his life, he will have to come to terms with the fact that the only way he can now go is down.

Peter Brown believes that John hasn't lost touch with what really matters in his life and he will not be left raging on the heath like King Lear. It is Brown's instinct that for John there *will* be a worthwhile life after No. 10, but he concedes that his predecessors have set dispiriting precedents. There is Edward Heath, a petulant old man consumed by bitterness; the ailing Harold Wilson, poignantly rooted in the past, beginning so many sentences with the phrase 'When I was Prime Minister . . . ': Margaret Thatcher, still pitifully trying to continue to exert influence over the nation from the House of Lords. But for John. Brown is sure, it will be different, because he *is* different.

Baroness Blatch says that Norma will be clear in her own mind how long she is prepared to soldier on with John in No. 10. She says that she is reconciled to the fact that he will require another term of office to implement his policies fully but, beyond that. she can't see her quietly sitting back and letting him go for a third term. If he loses the next General Election, she adds, Norma definitely will not want him staying on as Leader of the Opposition. Interestingly, she says that Norma will be very conscious of John's personal popularity, and, if it isn't high enough, she will be the first to tell him that it is time to step down.

A particularly testing time lies ahead for Norma in the next few years. Her children, her main concern for the past two decades. are now young adults (James is eighteen, Elizabeth twenty-one) and the continuing emphasis that she places on looking after them is beginning to seem very much like over-protectiveness. James has offered to board at Kimbolton, but Norma is against it, saying, somewhat unconvincingly, that the family can't afford it. Elizabeth has spoken about buying a flat in Huntingdon, but Norma is opposed to that idea, too, believing that at Finings she is at least safe, whereas in a flat on her own she could be easy prey for journalists or, far worse, kidnappers or terrorists.

Any mother who has been left to bring up her children on her own tends to form an unusually strong bond with them and often experiences problems letting go. In Norma's case, there is another reason why it could be especially difficult for her to come to terms with the idea of James and Elizabeth leaving home; once they have gone, she will be deprived of one of her best reasons for not living with her husband at No. 10. Some would no doubt say that the children's continuing presence provides her marriage with a useful façade.

Old friends like Baroness Blatch profess not to be worried about how Norma will adapt. She makes the point that she has adapted to every other change in her life, perhaps not immediately, perhaps not easily, but adapt she always has. Certainly Norma ought to be under no illusions that her children are both strong characters in their own right, both already starting to assert their independence. James decided not to go on the family holiday to Spain so that he could earn some money stacking shelves at a local chain store, even turned down a trip to Camp David because it clashed with a football fixture at school, and nobody has ever doubted that the fiery, headstrong Elizabeth can stand on her own two feet. Whether Norma likes it or not, Elizabeth and quite possibly James will feel the need to move away from home during the period that John is in office.

Baroness Blatch sees in the literary projects that Norma has already begun lining up an indication of a new metamorphosis. 'Norma the serious writer will soon be emerging,' she says. 'She has always had a good intellect. It often isn't obvious when a woman is playing the part of a wife or a mother, or maybe people don't look for it, but it will be apparent in this new role, believe me.' Guided by an experienced agent, Norma has already accepted lucrative commissions to update her Sutherland biography, and, taking full advantage of her position, consented to write *Chequers, The Illustrated Biography of a Country House*. The idea and the encouragement to write it came from Nesta Wyn Ellis. Norma's agent Andrew Lownie says it will be a book about Prime Ministers at rest and promises 'fascinating details' about her own life. Somewhat defensively, he insists that it will be no mere coffee-table book. There will be a great many words in it as well.

Virtually touting for business, Norma has let it be known in a newspaper interview that she would be interested in writing a screenplay for one of her favourite books, *The Way to the Lantern* by the late Audrey Erskine Lindop, which she had first read on her honeymoon. It is the story of an actor called Robert who evades the guillotine during the French Revolution by assuming different personae. The book would probably be prohibitively expensive to film, certainly for TV, but Vincent Shaw, who handles the rights to it, was struck by her realistic approach. (When they met to discuss the project just before the General Election, she told him: 'If we win we shall be busy, but I will find the time, but if we lose then no one will be interested, will they?')

The question, though, is what the public will make of Norma Major as a woman of letters. In this, as in every other role that she has tackled in her life, it will be approval which she will want more than anything, certainly more than financial reward or a place on the bestseller lists. It has to be said that the reviews for her book on Sutherland were not altogether encouraging, and, even if she does check her facts and her prose style is beyond reproach, she will still be laying herself open to the charge of cashing in on her husband's name. Edna Healey, a writer of unquestioned ability herself, says that the critics tend to have an immediate prejudice against anything that the wife of a public figure writes. Any slip will inevitably find its way into the gossip columns or *Private Eye*, indignities to which no other fledgling writer would normally be subjected. And, as Mary Wilson discovered whenever she published a volume of poetry, even if what she writes is successful, there is still the nagging doubt that the only reason anyone is interested in it is because of what her husband does for a living.

There is however no doubt that Norma's ancillary career as a writer has captured her imagination more than the duties of being the Prime Minister's wife. It was all too apparent when she decided not to accompany her husband to the G7 summit in Munich. Norma insists that she had decided 'months before' not to attend, but the Prime Minister's aides appeared to be taken by surprise. Some insisted right up until the last minute that she would be attending and others offered differing explanations as to why she wasn't there. They certainly seemed to have been expecting her in Munich; three bouquets were waiting at the hotel where the British delegation was staying, but only Judy Hurd and Rosemary Lamont were there to pick them up. The Prime Minister, unlike his two colleagues, had to wander in alone. His public image, increasingly, is becoming that of a solitary figure on the world stage.

With characteristic honesty, Norma finally told reporters in Britain that she absented herself in order to research her book about Chequers. At No. 10 a spokesman said, somewhat defensively: 'She just decided to stay at home and work – what's wrong with that?' Norma told Dulcie Atkins that there had been pressure on her to go – somebody from the Foreign Office had vainly drawn her attention to the fact that all the other leaders' wives were going, a busy programme had been drawn up for them, and she had, after all, been the hostess of the last G7 gathering – but, for her part, Norma didn't see the point. 'The wives aren't going to achieve anything,' she told Mrs Atkins.

'What is the point in spending the taxpayer's money in sending me along, too?' The press didn't see it in those terms. 'Major is minus his missus,' said a headline in the *Daily Mirror*, and a columnist on the *Evening Standard* wrote: 'I wonder if it is proper for Norma to pick and choose which prime ministerial events she attends. Perhaps it is. I just hope that she is not doing a Diana.' Comments like that annoy Norma intensely. As she says, 'I am not a paid public servant and can choose what I do and where I go.'

There was certainly no tut-tutting to be heard among the other cabinet wives at the time. Most of them had interests of their own: Louise Patten works as a client director at a City firm; Carolyn Portillo is a senior director at a leading firm of recruitment consultants; Caroline Waldegrave is managing director of Leith's, the London food college; Gail Lilley works as an artist; Patricia Newton is a part-time estate agent; Jean Mayhew is head of religious education at a girls' secondary school; and the list goes on. Among modern cabinet wives it has become almost *passé* for anyone to feel that she has to devote her entire life to trailing a few steps behind her husband. Judy Hurd says that she believes it is right and proper for Norma to profit from her position. It is not opportunism, she contends, it is hers as of right. All her life the political system has caused her to make sacrifices: this is the first occasion that she can use it to her own advantage.

Dulcie Atkins says that Norma is aware that there are certain occasions when her presence will not be requested, but required. 'She knows what you can go to and what you can't,' she says. For Norma, the 1992 Conservative Party Conference in Brighton was obviously a 'three-line whip' occasion, but few, if any, events could have paid more eloquent testimony to the fact that the party still regarded her as little more than a prop. Vanessa Ford, elevated to the position of the party's chief press officer, said tersely that Norma had no duties to perform 'in her own right' at the conference, except for a brief, informal walkabout among the trade stands on the first day. Anybody who watched Norma during conference week would certainly have appreciated why she would rather be doing other things with her time. To have seen her wandering around the trade stands, surrounded by her minders, being sought out and complimented by innumerable sycophants, trailed by reporters yearning for her to make a fool of herself, being earnestly lectured by businessmen who had no interest in her but who hoped that their company's name might appear in the background to the photographs, then going into the main hall and sitting through the interminable speeches, surreptitiously looking at her watch, stifling a yawn, then a big, impersonal lunch for some organisation or other, then more speeches to sit through in the afternoon, then dinner, then, no doubt, waiting some hours for John in their hotel suite . . . that was to get a real flavour of what it is like to be Norma Major going to the aid of the party.

That December when she accompanied John to Canada, the strain did get too much for her. After she failed to turn up at a State banquet, John had to give an explanation to reporters: travel sickness. 'She is a bad traveller,' he said. 'She is feeling much better now although I had some difficulty waking her this morning.'

There has been a great deal of press speculation about how Norma is about to emerge as some kind of housewife-superstar, barnstorming around the world fighting for the causes which she believes in, talking at grand functions and making her mark on the public consciousness in the manner of Hillary Clinton, who said she wanted to be known not as the First Lady but as 'the presidential partner'. Norma's own office has been heightening the anticipation by putting out statements saying that she is 'considering the role', and saying that she looked upon her first eighteen months as the Prime Minister's wife as a 'rehearsal' period. The implication of what friends like Mrs Atkins are saying is that Norma will in fact be doing as little as she possibly can of the duties of the Prime Minister's wife, and that all those who are expecting a dazzling performance after such a long period of rehearsal will be sadly disappointed.

Norma has obviously given the matter a considerable amount of thought. When she discussed it with Harvey Thomas, he told her that there is no such thing as 'the role of the Prime Minister's wife'. She is just a woman who happens to be married to the Prime Minister and how she comes to terms with it is entirely up to her. She oughtn't to feel guilty about not doing it 'properly' because nobody has ever defined a right way to do it. At the party conference in Brighton, when she found herself the first-ever Prime Minister's wife to be accorded a standing ovation, she might have reflected that although Britain had seen more formidable women in her role in the past, for none of them had the role been quite so formidable as it had been for her.

Norma has been in touch with all her surviving predecessors – Ladies Eden, Wilson and Callaghan – and has seen from their experiences that being the wife of a Prime Minister is very much what you make of it. Clarissa Eden, at thirty-four the youngest Prime Minister's wife that the country has seen in this century, probably had the most to offer of the three: 'Lady Eden combines beauty, brains and the modern outlook,' said a headline in a newspaper called the *Bulletin* (such deference to a Prime Minister's wife seems almost quaint by today's standards of reporting). She found, however, that during her brief period in No. 10 playing her own part in public life was eminently less important than nursing her seriously ill husband through the dark days of the Suez crisis, and, accordingly, the public got to see little, if anything, of her. In her own way, she none the less performed an undeniably valuable service for her country.

For Norma, Mary Wilson's story ought to serve as a cautionary tale. She ended up being miserable as the Prime Minister's wife because she failed to assert herself. She never got on top of the role – it just got on top of her. No great feminist, she sat silently in the background, hating politics and the life that she had to lead.

disliking many of her husband's acquaintances, playing the dutiful, dull, decent little wife and reportedly having to put up with being bossed around by Sir Harold's right-hand woman, the imperious Lady Falkender. To her friends, Mrs Wilson used to complain that she had a terrible feeling that life was passing her by. She found it difficult to set aside time for her own interests, such as her poetry, and seemed to spend all of her time waiting to see her husband, who, on the rare occasions when she did get to see him, seemed preoccupied and distracted. In Harold's memoirs she appears only fleetingly, and during his time in office he took her very much for granted. It was only after he had relinquished his power that, like King Lear, he regained his perspective on life. When everyone else had left him, Mary stayed true, nursing him lovingly through ill health in his dotage.

Her successor, Audrey Callaghan, is a better role model by far for Norma because she had the strength of character to carry on with her life more or less as normal after her husband became Prime Minister. She also had a splendidly positive outlook on life. She continued to chair the board of governors of Great Ormond Street Hospital for Sick Children in London, even when it brought her into conflict with the unions during the 1979 hospital workers' strike. She was unfazed by journalists and would always speak to them with a disarming honesty which earned her their respect. She had no qualms about talking about political matters – she said that she was horrified by the hospital workers' strike, and, on another occasion, said publicly: 'We all have our moans about rising prices. I expect Jim has been fed up with me telling him how quickly the money goes these days.' A tall, commanding woman, she was once famously described by a friend as 'ten times the man Jim is'. It was she who dusted her husband down and got him back on his feet again after his two greatest political setbacks – first when he was dropped from the Labour Party's national executive and again in 1967 after devaluation.

As Norma's immediate predecessor, it is extraordinary how much more freedom she had enjoyed. Nobody ever told her what to do or what to say, not least because they sensed that she was not the kind of woman who would take too kindly to it. She says that she could walk around more or less as she pleased and it was a matter of supreme indifference to Special Branch what she did with her time. She tells the story of how she once caught a bus with her granddaughter who told the conductor very proudly that her grandmother lived in No. 10. Much to her amusement, he gave the little girl a clip round the ear for being cheeky. The press gave Mrs Callaghan a much easier time of it too. Even in the most ardently Conservative newspapers she was well liked. 'Oh, lucky Jim – just to have a devoted wife like Audrey,' said a headline in the *Daily Express*. 'The perfect partner,' said the *Daily Mail*. The *Daily Mirror* probably put it best when it described her as 'a down-to-earth, no-nonsense, roast beef and Yorkshire pudding sort of lady'.

Towards the end of her husband's premiership, Lady Callaghan found herself subjected to a kind of criticism that she had never had to face before. The *Daily Express* columnist Jean Rook, pioneering a form of journalism now commonplace, decided to attack Mrs Callaghan for the clothes she wore when she accompanied her husband to a heads of government conference in the Caribbean. 'Where in the back of her airing cupboard did Audrey dig up that cotton sun frock?' wrote the self-styled 'First Lady of Fleet Street'. 'Sleeveless, shapeless, floral, scoop-necked and three inches too long, I've never seen anything like it.' Lady Callaghan remembers the piece. It struck her at the time as unnecessary and rude, quite unlike anything that she'd had to put up with before. That piece, innocuous by today's standards, nevertheless marked the beginning of a difficult new era in relations between prime ministerial wives and the press.

It was not just a more critical, but also a far more probing and insatiable press which Norma found lying in wait for her when

John became Prime Minister twelve years later. She was almost certainly the first Prime Minister's wife to be asked – by Nesta Wyn Ellis – if she felt satisfied that her husband was making love to her enough times ('Well, I suppose enough,' she had replied.) More column inches were devoted to Norma during her first three months as the Prime Minister's wife than her three surviving predecessors had had put together. Her life story was subjected to a degree of scrutiny unheard of in the past. Within days of her husband entering the Conservative Party leadership contest, a reporter from one national newspaper had tracked down, in the wilds of Shropshire, several people who had known her parents during the Second World War. At St Catherine's House in London others had got out almost all the marriage and birth certificates relating to her past, hoping to find, presumably, a whiff of scandal in the family. Rightly or wrongly, the Prime Minister's wife has come to be seen as fair game.

Norma has paradoxically fanned press interest by so often declining requests for interviews. It is doubtful whether newspapers would have been interested in assigning reporters to investigate her background had she been prepared to talk about it herself. She merely invited speculation that she had a skeleton in her closet. She will probably never understand the inhabitants of Fleet Street and they are unlikely ever to understand her. That she can quote from memory just about every negative comment that they have made about her over the years shows just how deeply they have wounded her. She took exception to, among other things, a report which stated that she wore white plastic boots when she met her husband (they were actually leather), the use of the word 'indifferent' to describe the food which was served at one of her New Year's Eve parties, and, of course, the many barbs directed at the blue suit which she wore two days running after John won the leadership election.

As catty and uncalled for as all the remarks are, they are still, it has to be said, mere flesh wounds compared to what Glenys Kinnock, for one, had to endure almost every day she was married to the leader of the opposition. (Elizabeth Smith, her bookish successor, stays at home in Scotland and has so far succeeded in keeping a remarkably low profile. Her real test will come at the next General Election.) What Norma appears to find so needling is that there is a common thread running through almost all the hostile pieces being written about her: that she didn't come from the right social class and didn't quite know the right way to do things.

Naively perhaps, Norma seems to apply to journalists the same standards of behaviour which her mother instilled in her as a child: if you can't think of something nice to say about someone, don't say anything. One report which appeared in the *Today* newspaper, claiming that she was having the private quarters at No. 10 redecorated at the taxpayers' expense, so incensed her that she took the unusual step of asking the No. 10 press office to request a correction ('Mr and Mrs Major have asked us to point out . . . ' it cheekily began).

Her relationship with the Fourth Estate hasn't been helped by her often muddle-headed dealings with its representatives. She agonised over whether to do a fashion shoot for Terry O'Neill in the *Tatler*, did it, thought twice about it, and then contacted the editor, Jane Procter, asking her to withdraw some of the pictures because she felt that in a recession it was inappropriate to be seen to be wearing such expensive clothes and jewellery. The magazine agreed to her requests but, to her horror, used her as their 'cover girl'. The picture showed a woman who had made a breath-taking transformation, but there was a strangely vacant look in her eyes. She seemed to be the typical *Tatler* model: hair by Ian Denson, make-up by Barbara Daly, personality to be arranged. Norma's friend Fred Heddell, the chief executive of Mencap, discovered quite what a sore point the picture had been with her when he innocently made a joke about it. 'She clearly wasn't happy about it,' he says. 'She didn't see that sort of thing as her role or the way that she wished to portray herself.' In the event, the pictures of Norma (there were more inside) were well received in Fleet Street where there was a lot of wishful talk about how she finally seemed to have turned over a new leaf. The only discordant note was struck by Anne Robinson in the *Daily Mirror* who observed that the Nicole Farhi, Mulberry and Jasper Conran outfits which she wore all unhappily took on the Windsmoor look when Norma put them on.

Norma's friends still talk of how bitterly she regretted seeing Nesta Wyn Ellis for her biography of John Major. As much as Norma complained about it afterwards, the author insists that she had sent her a copy of the manuscript to make corrections, but Norma had failed to return it in time for the deadline. Miss Wyn Ellis adds that she had already agreed to one or two requests from the press office at No. 10 to delete several comments which Norma had made which in hindsight were unhelpful politically, but her principal sin, as far as Norma herself was concerned, appeared to be in faithfully reporting a comment which Robert Atkins had made about how John did not talk about his career in front of her. Norma subsequently denied that this was the case. Pat Dessoy says that what hurt Norma most of all was the fact that she had actually liked Wyn Ellis and saw what she did as a betrayal of her trust and even friendship. She believed, quaintly, that Wyn Ellis was taking such an interest in her because she was a friend, rather than a highly skilled interviewer.

Mrs Dessoy says, interestingly, that part of Norma's problem with the media is her 'innate honesty'. She notes, for example, that there was no reason why she should have told the press that she was born Norma Wagstaff, thereby raising the awkward question of why her mother was called Mrs Johnson. By contrast, in John Major's entry in *Who's Who*, Norma's name at birth is given as Johnson, as it is in Debrett's *Distinguished People of Today*, where it is also erroneously stated that Norma's father was killed in action.

For this book, Norma organised two interviews several months apart and cancelled them both at the last minute, saying she felt it was 'too early' for her biography to be written.

Peter Brown, a man who admits, with some courage, to finding *Spitting Image* perfectly acceptable, has tried to bring Norma into a closer relationship with the media. 'I have said to her that when the press wants to do something, for God's sake let them do it, and let them get it out of their system, and then you'll find they won't bother you again after that,' he says. The newspaper revelations about David Mellor's affair with the actress Antonia de Sancha have served only to harden her attitude – Mellor himself still speaks bitterly about the 'sadistic' nature of a large number of journalists. After the calls for Norman Lamont's resignation, Norma seemed finally to have despaired of the media and asked Dulcie Atkins: 'I wonder who they will go for next . . . they're gradually making their way through the entire cabinet, aren't they?'

Even more unforgivable, for Norma, has been the way that the media have targeted her own children. She can point to in-numerable examples. They made Elizabeth burst into tears as they pleaded with her to talk to them after a performance with the Huntingdon Youth Band. James's perfectly normal relation-ship with a local girl became a page lead in several of the tabloids, and subsequently a report about him being sent off for foul play during a school football match made the front page of the *Daily Telegraph*. That seems to her even more insidious. Dulcie Atkins says that the fact that it didn't make the front pages of any of the other broadsheets and only made page four of the *Sun* fuelled Norma's suspicions that its prominence might have had something to do with James's father's unhappy relationship with the *Telegraph*. They seemed to be using his son's foul as further evidence that the Majors were 'bad stock'. 'James himself was furious about that,' says Mrs Atkins. 'Norma gets a hundred times more upset when the press pick on her children than when they pick on her and John.'

For all the trials and tribulations of being married to the Prime Minister, Norma has found that there are at least some compensations. There have been meetings with members of the glitterati such as Luciano Pavarotti, whom she saw after his rain-swept performance in Hyde Park, and Frank Sinatra, whom she sat next to at a dinner after his performance at the Royal Albert Hall. That was, says Baroness Blatch, 'a great thrill' for her, but Norma was annoyed when some of the reporters covering the event went with the angle that the old crooner kept her and John waiting while he showered after the performance. Norma has also found that she is starting to enjoy the travelling a little more. On her trip to China and Moscow, she confided a girlish excitement at feeling 'a part of history'.

Barbara Wallis, Norma's secretary at No. 10, recalls her delight when she received a letter from the producer of a regional TV programme called *The Help Squad*, which inquired whether she would be interested in going to St Buryan in Cornwall to ring some bells which were, reputedly, the heaviest in the world. 'My goodness, that sounds like fun,' Norma exclaimed. 'Let's do it.' It had apparently occurred to very few people who wrote to her – all those worthies who were wanting her to cut ribbons, be a patron of a charity, or open a school – to ask themselves the simple question: Is this something that Mrs Major is actually likely to *enjoy*?

Chris Donat, presenter of *The Help Squad*, was pleasantly surprised when she consented. No. 10 didn't generally accede to requests from regional TV programmes, particularly not a programme like his, which involved Donat turning up in Downing Street to interview her dressed as a 'wacky pizza delivery man'. But Donat says that Norma was a delight to talk to, and, when they got down to St Buryan, her sense of excitement was obvious, like a schoolgirl let out for a field trip. 'This was obviously something very different for her,' says Donat. 'She went into it expecting to have fun and she did.' Norma told him that she'd had a passionate interest in campanology ever since she had read about it as a girl in a Dorothy L. Sayers mystery, *The Nine Tailors*. She had been a member of a group at St Ives, but, over the past few years, had become a little out of practice, 'what with one thing and another'. Donat describes it as a magical day. 'I'd feared it might have been a bit stiff and formal, but Norma went out of her way to put everyone at their ease and in fact made sure everyone enjoyed it as much as she did,' says Donat. There was just one hitch: when they filmed her arriving at the old village church, Donat jumped out of the car without putting the handbrake on and left the Prime Minister's wife rolling back down the hill. She fortunately had the presence of mind to apply the handbrake before it reached the main road (but not soon enough, alas, to prevent the outtake being dispatched to *It'll Be Alright on the Night*).

Another source of enjoyment for Norma turned out to be Chequers. Belatedly taking Lady Wilson's advice, she fell in love with the Tudor mansion on her first visit: 'It's like an overgrown country cottage, very welcoming, warm and comfortable,' she said. She and John spend weekends there about once every two months and invitations to their Sunday lunches are coveted among their friends and courtiers. 'They are very laid back, very informal affairs,' says David Mellor. 'I suppose they are just larger versions of the kind of Sunday lunch which ordinary people have up and down the country.' The MP William Hague says that Norma has personally shown him some of the house's many treasures — a painting by Constable, the ring worn by Queen Elizabeth I and letters written by Napoleon from St Helena among them — and says that she speaks with awe of the sense of history which pervades the building. She says that she has made it her objective to sleep in every four-poster bed in the building before John leaves No. 10.

During the seventy-five years that the house has been used by the nation's Prime Ministers, it has been rare for invitations to be extended beyond members of the Privy Council and their immediate families. John and Norma have introduced a new kind of people to the historic pile – their friends. Rosemary Juggins, an early guest, says that the Majors have been systematically inviting just about all their closest friends from their days in Lambeth and Huntingdon. Norma told Mrs Juggins to arrive early on the Saturday that she had been asked to come (guests normally don't arrive until around midday) so she would have time to show her around. Norma's sense of wonder was evident to Mrs Juggins as she took her on a guided tour of the building. 'There was nothing proprietorial about the way she did it, we were just two friends looking over this marvellous old building,' says Mrs Juggins. 'It was quite a giggle.'

Norma has had a variety of showbusiness stars, including Sir Harry Secombe and, predictably, Dame Joan Sutherland, to stay, and, no doubt confirming the worst fears of some of her husband's more snobbish critics, another of Norma's guests was Ian Denson, unquestionably the first hairdresser ever to have lunched at Chequers. He says that he was taken by surprise when the official invitation arrived. He had attended to Norma just days before and she hadn't mentioned it, but it was certainly very much on his mind when she next visited the salon. 'I said to her "Thank you very much for the invitation. Rachel [Pryce, a fellow hairdresser] and I are absolutely delighted and we are really looking forward to it."' Norma replied: 'Oh you *are* coming. Well, that's terrific because we are both looking forward to having you.' On the big day, Ian walked into the dining room and saw about half a dozen tables laid out. To his delight, he found that Rachel and he were on Norma's table and they had a chance over drinks beforehand to talk to John too. 'When people meet him in person he is a very different man from the way he comes across on the television,' he says. 'He and Norma were very good hosts. They do that job in the way that any married couple hosting a luncheon would host such an occasion. I think that it is really nice that they have opened the place up to people that they like. Rachel and I were very flattered and proud to have been able to go there and I think our mothers were even more excited about it than we were.'

Even the elder statesmen on the Majors' guest list – Lord Callaghan and Edward Heath – would never have made it past the threshold in Mrs Thatcher's day, and even though Mrs Thatcher did knight him, she never wished to take lunch with the actor and gay rights campaigner Ian McKellen, as the Majors did. For all the guests at Chequers, it was Norma rather than John who looked after them. The weekend Mrs Juggins was there, John, very typically, didn't arrive until the early hours of Saturday morning and didn't surface until lunchtime, when he was feeling decidedly groggy. During the afternoon and again after dinner he retired to the White Room (his office) to go through his official papers, and then he had to return to London early on Sunday afternoon. 'They went to the local church in the morning, but without any great enthusiasm,' said another guest. 'That is one tradition neither of them is very fond of.'

A number of guests spoke of how strange it seemed to see John and Norma in such an august setting. One man, who has been a regular visitor under the past three premiers, said, 'You go though all the security checks, drive up that marvellous drive-way, get greeted at the door by that splendid old housekeeper, have your bags taken up to your room by uniformed stewards, and then you walk down through the Palladian arcade to the Great Hall for pre-lunch drinks, and there, in the middle of the crowd, are John and Norma, looking for all the world as if they were having a bit of a do in a semi in Surbiton. I must say that I found it really rather delightful.'

It became clear to Norma that Chequers was more than just a place to show off to her friends. She realised that the kudos attached to it could be converted into hard cash for her pet charity, Mencap, which was, in the early days of John's premier-ship, in rather poor shape in terms of its morale. She initiated a meeting with Fred Heddell, the charity's progressive new chief executive at their headquarters near the Barbican, and told him that he could discreetly let it be known that people who made donations to the charity at 'a certain level' would be rewarded by receiving an invitation to Chequers. Once the word got out, her offer was taken up with considerable enthusiasm, despite the fact that each invitation was effectively retailing at around £5,000 a time. It was a little more than it cost to stay at the run-of-the-mill country house hotel, but then, as Norma had realised, there was nothing run-of-the-mill about Chequers. 'She made sure that such guests enjoyed themselves, but left them under no illusions as to why they were there,' says Lord Rix, Mencap's chairman. 'In fact I would actually be brought on sometimes to spell it out.'

By happy coincidence, Mencap gave Norma an excuse to bring opera to Chequers. A series of gala fundraising events held in the building brought in still more money for the charity – there were two Pavilion operas and a concert of music by Donizetti, which alone raised more than £120,000, thanks largely to contribu-tions from the Jewish community. A record £560,000 was made at another operatic evening attended by just 100 people. One businessman flew in from Hong Kong for the occasion with five guests and told the organisers that he considered it such good value for money that he would be coming again next year. Heddell admits that Norma had raised not just money but also a number of eyebrows by using Chequers in this way. 'The trustees of Chequers are not mad about the current arrangement, but Norma feels that so long as we keep it to a reasonable level, we'll get away with it,' he says.

A dinner for businessmen organised at No. 10 under Norma's auspices boosted the charity's coffers still further, and it was on that occasion that Norma met the distributors of a forthcoming Tom Cruise film, *Far and Away*, and persuaded them to open it at a charity première in London in aid of Mencap. She wisely decided that half the proceeds should be given to another charity, Relate, the marriage guidance organisation, to demonstrate that she wasn't showing Mencap too much favouritism. For the big occasions, such as the film première, Heddell says that Norma made sure that John was there – another happy coincidence, he feels, because his presence was useful for the charity, and useful for the Prime Minister politically. 'She does not look for personal accolades, but John does tend to,' he says. 'When people thank them publicly for their work for the charity, she always looks embarrassed and he always looks very proud.'

There are other less conspicuous ways in which Norma helps raise money for Mencap. Lord Rix, its chairman, recalls a private lunch which she got John to accompany her to at Lord Archer's cottage in Grantchester. Rix says that apart from himself and his wife Elspet and the Majors and the Archers, there were several Japanese gentlemen at the table, whose presence was initially a mystery to him. It turned out that Archer had been tying up some deal with them to publish his books in their country, and had mentioned it to Norma, and together they had decided that, with the Prime Minister in attendance, their visitors might be encouraged to give some money to Mencap too while they were over. 'Let's be honest about it,' says Rix. 'At the end of it all we received some substantial contributions to the charity, which were, of course, more than welcome.'

Heddell believes that Norma is worth £1 million to Mencap during each financial year that her husband is in No. 10. 'During the first year I was chief executive, that made the difference between me being able to balance the books and not being able to,' he says. 'Or, put another way, it saved me from having to make £1 million-worth of people at Mencap redundant.' He says that he is conscious that other charities have seen Norma's value and occasionally they try to muscle in, but she has so far remained remarkably loyal. He has tried formalising the arrangement by offering her a grander title than merely being a patron, but she has declined. 'We've got the Queen Mum as our royal patron and if we are honest she is not a great deal of use these days,' he says. 'Norma has filled the gap for us.'

Looking at it coldly and calculatingly, Rix says, Princess Diana is probably the most valuable patron a charity can have, but he reckons Norma is probably the next best thing. It was in fact noticeable at the *Far and Away* première that more photographers were taking pictures of Princess Diana, Relate's patron, than they were of Norma (but then more pictures still were taken that night of David Mellor's publicity-seeking former mistress Antonia de Sancha, which shows that there is no accounting for taste).

Although Norma doesn't have the cachet of a royal, she does have the keys to Chequers and No. 10, and she can also involve the Prime Minister in the charity's activities. Rix says: 'She gets him to go along to our events which of course shows that she influences him in our favour, but I would hesitate to use her pillow talk to our advantage. I don't think that would be right. I am very aware of the fact that I should never write a letter to her at No. 10 begging her to get her husband to do something for us. Of course we talk from time to time and she might offer to do something and I might say "What a good idea," but I think that's different.'

Heddell says that as the Prime Minister's wife, her involvement with Mencap shows a considerable streak of independence because the charity has a political role fighting for the rights of mentally-handicapped people which it exercises without fear or favour. 'We have raised a few hackles among politicians in the Tory Party,' he says. 'Norma is definitely not a political animal. She is certainly not protective of the government or the Tory Party either privately or publicly.'

Wearing her charity hats, Norma finds it all too easy to become embroiled in controversy. She was at loggerheads with the health minister Dr Brian Mawhinney after leading a campaign to raise £150,000 to help build a home for Mencap in a residential area in Peterborough. Mawhinney, who also happens to be the local MP, opposed the plan because people in the neighbourhood objected to the increased traffic which they believed the home would generate. Norma went to see the residents to listen to what they had to say, but summarily rejected their case.

On another occasion Norma withdrew her patronage from the charity Music for the World, which planned to raise cash for environmental causes, after it was disclosed in the newspapers that only 10 per cent of the £110,000 it had collected had found its way to green projects. (Nesta Wyn Ellis, who had encouraged her to become involved, says she was annoyed that she pulled out immediately after the stories appeared in the press, without troubling to find out the details for herself). These were two relatively inconsequential stories, but both made the headlines because of the Major name.

Many of Norma's friends are unusually coy on the question of what influence she has on John. 'We're moving into an area here that it's best we keep out of,' Peter Golds says. John himself, like almost all married men who hold high political office, seems to want it both ways. On the one hand, he is loath to give anyone the impression that he subscribes to the Victorian notion that he believes his wife should be seen and not heard. And yet he would probably hate it even more if anyone suggested that his wife might have the impudence to sway his hand on matters of policy. He wouldn't want to lay himself open to the same sort of attacks that Neil Kinnock had to face, not least from Edwina Currie, who once suggested, notoriously, that he was the man who had his breakfast cooked for him in the mornings by the leader of the opposition.

During the election campaign Norma dutifully made it clear that she was a wife who knew her place. 'I don't really under-stand policies,' she said meekly in one interview. 'John and I rarely discuss politics, and if I ever want to know something, I sometimes get a sharp answer.' Such sentiments are anathema to feminists, but at the time she had good reason to express them. It gave Central Office and the newspapers assisting them during the campaign a clear shot at Glenys Kinnock.

It would of course be a peculiar marriage if Norma did *not* have any influence at all over her husband. She regularly shares the same bed as the Prime Minister, which is rather more, as Barbara Wallis wryly observes, than even his principal private secretary has ever achieved. Baroness Blatch's frank remarks about how Norma wouldn't be prepared to sit back and let John go for a third full term show that she is not as passive as she has sometimes been made out to be. Miss Wallis says: 'Sometimes John would take a view on something, and, after talking to Norma about it, would adopt a mellower line. I don't think that should be a secret. As I see it, one of the most useful roles a Prime Minister's spouse can play is to try to keep on living as ordinary a life as possible and talking to ordinary people, and communicating what she sees and hears to the Prime Minister. That can be an indispensable safety gauge.'

As to Norma's beliefs, the signals are a shade confusing. On the issues which stir the masses, such as capital punishment, she is in favour – instinctively, she says, if not rationally. She is just as keen on corporal punishment; nobody, she declares, has the right to tell her whether she can or cannot smack her children. The idea of a 'nanny state' is objectionable to her. Although she accepts that her own life has been somewhat cloistered, she said once: 'I've not got much time for . . . people who sit back and say I'm not going to be accepted because I'm black or a woman.' That and the fact that she has given up listening to the Radio 4 *Today* programme because she considers it too left-wing for her tastes again points to someone on the right, if not the far right, but that is not the whole picture. On many social issues, she says that she is 'on the damp side'. Having friends from such a wide cross-section of society, quite a few of them Socialists, she is well aware what unemployment means to individual families and that is the issue generally reckoned to be of greatest concern to her. She has spoken movingly about the plight of individuals who have been made unemployed to Gillian Shephard, the employment minister and a long-standing luncheon companion of hers. As Olive Baddeley says: 'When Norma picks up a paper and reads about a crisis on the money market or some company collapsing, it isn't the politics of it that concerns her – it is the fact that ordinary people's lives are being affected.'

There is also a theory that Norma, having known so many homosexuals herself in her younger days, was instrumental in persuading John to take the unprecedented step of meeting Sir Ian McKellen at No. 10 to talk about homosexual rights. She had already got him on to the luncheon list at Chequers and had told a number of her friends how much she had admired him and the work he was doing. For Sir Ian, himself unaware of any involvement by Norma, it could explain one mystery: he had been struck by the fact that the Prime Minister, having professed himself far from familiar with the subject, used one or two words at the meeting which required specialist knowledge of the problems that homosexuals were facing. For Christmas, John bought James a copy of the late Freddie Mercury's *Bohemian Rhapsody* and had his press office put out a statement saying that he was 'delighted' that the profits being made from sales of the record were going towards fighting AIDS. 'Mr Major believes the profits are going to a very worthy cause.' said his spokesman.

Norma's hand has occasionally been detected in the honours lists. The OBE for the make-up artist Barbara Daly almost certainly came about on her recommendation. Her interest in opera seemed to be reflected in Elisabeth Schwarzkopf and Margaret Price being made Dames. John Thaw, the star of one of her favourite TV series, *Inspector Morse*, received a CBE. It is also considered likely that, on Norma's advice, a further honour will probably be forthcoming for June Bronhill during John's premiership (she already has the OBE). It would be wrong to suggest that Norma always gets her way, however. She was by all accounts not too keen on the idea of a peerage for Jeffrey Archer,

'She's no fan of Jeffrey's, is she?' says Fred Heddell) but John, much taken by the man, evidently chose to disregard her, so Lord Archer of Weston-super-Mare it was.

Most of the time, Norma does not have to try to influence John because they tend to think alike. Unlike the Reagans and the Thatchers, there is no dominant partner in the relationship. John and Norma are, as Olive Baddeley says, 'two of a kind'. It is still useful that Norma occasionally has her say. Within No. 10, it is easy for John, as any Prime Minister, to lose touch. Robert Atkins says that he has seen a change in the way people treat John now that he is the Prime Minister: 'There are a lot of people who have suddenly started to agree with him on just about everything, which I feel is worrying,' he says. There was an occasion, so it is said, when John went into a cabinet meeting and purposely told a joke which didn't make sense to see if anybody laughed. It worried him too that just about everybody did.

Audrey Callaghan had sensed the pernicious dangers of the 'yes-men' herself during her husband's tenure of No. 10. She always felt that, as the one person in her husband's entourage who didn't have to worry about such things as career prospects, it was important for her to give her opinions on matters of policy when her husband solicited them, because she knew that, from her at least, he would be getting an honestly held opinion. For that reason it was, as she saw it, almost her *duty* to speak her mind. That Denis Thatcher to some extent abdicated that responsibility for a quiet life might well have been one of the reasons why his wife became so disastrously out of touch in her final years.

Norma has certainly fought hard to keep her feet and those of her family planted firmly on the ground, even as her husband pulled them up with him into conditions of zero gravity. Her strongest grip on the real world had always been through her friends. The friends who mean the most to her are the ones who have been there from the beginning, for she can be sure they like her for what she is as opposed to her new-found status. In an increasingly complex and unfamiliar world, she feels the need to surround herself with as many of them as she can. Her former secretary at No. 10, Barbara Wallis (latterly succeeded by Lorne Roper-Caldbeck), is a friend of the Lambeth vintage, as is Peter Brown. Sometimes, it seems, Norma has a real problem letting go. When she saw Andrew Thomson at a party at No. 10 after the General Election, she implored him to introduce her to the new crop of Tory party agents. 'I said, "Norma, I'm retired, I don't know these kids, you need somebody more in touch,"' Thomson recalls. 'But she was adamant. "No, no, you don't understand, Andrew, I would feel happier if *you* were to do it."'

Many people whom Norma had known for years inevitably began to behave differently towards her after her husband had got into No. 10. Some would sign their letters 'yours sincerely' when, in the old days, they would have put 'love'. One or two took down the pictures of John and Norma which they had on their walls because they felt that their friends would think that they were swanking or making some kind of political point. 'You oughtn't to regard your friends as trophies,' says Alicia Hollings (née Gains). Others spoke of how they consciously limited the number of times they got in touch because they felt that the Majors had reached a stage in their lives when they would have better things to do than talk to them. 'I don't like to intrude any more,' says Rosemary Juggins. 'I certainly feel that Norma won't want to be bothered by me. I've no longer got anything to offer her.' Margaret Marshall says: 'I would have got in touch with them both if John had lost the election, but, as things turned out, I thought that it would be best to let them be. What could I say that could possibly be of interest to them?'

Ironically, Norma is often by herself at Finings, yearning for a friend to call. The isolation and loneliness that can go with power repels her. She is always at pains to point out to her friends that the giant bomb-proof gates which the police put up outside her home aren't intended to keep any of them out. Pat Wheeler, Bernard Perkins's ex-wife, says that she saw her for the first time in some years recently at a party at Peter Brown's house and couldn't help but behave deferentially towards her when she came up to have a chat. 'I could tell that was not what Norma wanted and she started talking with some determination about ordinary things, as if she was still in Lambeth. She seemed to be saying: "Look, I'm just the same, please don't treat me any differently."'

Just as some of the Majors' closest friends feel the need to back away, so a great many others who aren't their friends in any real sense have started drawing close. They are what Lady Wilson used to call the 'fair-weather friends', a parasitic life-form that has long been prevalent in No. 10. They attach themselves to the Prime Minister, his wife and his children so long as the power remains, but extricate themselves the moment it disappears. Olive Baddeley says that Norma, a good judge of character, has already identified all the fair-weather friends that her husband has attracted. 'There are a lot of people, some of them quite famous, who would be very surprised indeed to know what Norma privately thought about them,' she says. 'I have been at functions with her when some chap has come up and made a big fuss of her, and, when he's finally walked away, she's whispered in my ear "Patronising s***."' Fred Heddell, Mencap's chief executive, says: 'Norma is utterly charming to people when she is with them at functions. You only pick up afterwards that she might find some of them extremely irksome. I was at a fundraising event at No. 10 with her once and she came up to me and got hold of my arm and said, "Can we get away from all these people?"'

When Norma is attending luncheons and dinners, she always insists that she is seated next to somebody she knows. For Mencap functions, Lord Rix says that that means either himself of his wife Elspet, Fred Heddell or his wife Jill or Lord Renton. Norma is understandably wary of people who have suddenly wished to befriend her during her husband's premiership and has added very few to her close coterie. One or two have joined her list of regular luncheon companions – among them, Carole

Stone, the former *Any Questions?* producer, who also got an invitation to Chequers, along with her boyfriend Richard Lindley – and, touchingly, she has also struck up a very real friendship with Heather Strudwick, the lady in the iron lung whom she met at the reception at No. 10, along with her sister, Patricia Crittenden. She has written to them both frequently. During the summer, she agreed to attend a garden party Heather gave, but had to pull out at the last minute because of another engagement. To make up for not being there herself, she pulled a few strings to have a group of Morris dancers perform at the event. Heather, a lady very keen on Morris dancers, says that she was tickled pink. 'It's marvellous really that she should bother with organising a little treat for me when she has got so many other things on her mind.' she says.

Norma's defences tend to go up when strangers try to ingratiate themselves. At the Commonwealth Summit in Harare, Hella Pick, the diplomatic editor of the *Guardian*, walked up to her and said: 'It is high time that you and I ceased to be strangers.' Norma replied: 'Don't worry, I am quite happy with things just as they are.'

It amuses Robert Atkins whenever he picks up a book about John Major to see people who have hardly made his acquaintance passing themselves off as life-long friends of the family. and. invariably, talking all sorts of nonsense about them. During the course of his research, the author of this book took a number of unsolicited telephone calls from surprisingly well-known figures who wanted to be interviewed. Their unseemly desire to see their names in the index demonstrated what social and political oneupmanship is to be had in being seen to be a friend of the Prime Minister's wife.

In this topsy-turvy world. it is hardly surprising that Norma has always been so fiercely loyal to her real friends. There are legions of stories about her dropping everything at No. 10 to go to friends whom she has heard are unwell or in need of help. Lord Rix. seriously ill recently with heart problems. says that he was enormously touched by the concern that Norma showed for him – writing, telephoning, sending cards all the time. 'It was very typical of her,' he says. Pre Newbon, a friend of Norma's from Huntingdon, bumped into her outside Hinchingbroke Hospital where she was visiting two local councillors whom she knew well and who were recovering from operations. 'She is doing things like that all the time, but nobody ever hears about them,' says Mrs Newbon. 'I am amazed the way she manages to fit it all in.' When Emily Blatch became a Baroness, Norma dressed her up a little teddy bear in all the robes of her rank and presented it to her. And when Norma heard that Barbara Wallis's cat had died, she brought her back a china lookalike from Rhodesia to console her.

When John was putting in calls of support to David Mellor when his private life was being splashed over the front pages of the tabloids, Norma thought immediately of his wife, Judy, and put in calls to console *her*. 'She just wanted me to know that she was there for me,' says Mrs Mellor. 'She hated what the press were doing to my husband and wanted to make it clear that she would remain friends with me no matter what happened. I was very touched.' And when Clare Latimer found herself in the media spotlight after John announced that he was going to sue over the allegations about his private life, Norma, typically, let it be known that Latimer still had her friendship and that they had lunched together.

Above all, Norma has never neglected her children. At the Huntingdon Steeplechases, when Elizabeth fell off her mount during her first race in public, Norma immediately ran out on to the track, just like any good mother would have done, to see if she was all right. With the photographers and bodyguards and course officials circling around her, she sat on the grass beside her daughter watching anxiously as a Red Cross nurse attended to her. After a few agonisingly long minutes, Norma's terrified expression finally gave way to a broad smile when the nurse informed her that her daughter had suffered nothing more than a few bruises. At that moment, it was never more obvious what mattered to Norma Major and what didn't.

Epilogue

EBRUARY 1993: New South Wales, Australia. Mrs Bette Caunt kisses her husband Peter goodbye as he sets off for work from their beach-front bungalow. It is a marvellously hot summer's day. Mrs Caunt and her youngest daughter Julia decide to take a morning dip.

Life couldn't be better for the Caunts. They moved to Australia from Britain in 1981 after Peter resigned as the operations manager for Great Manchester's transport department. In New South Wales he soon found work with a local bus company where he now works as the general manager. He is fifty-five, tall, well-built, with dark hair and an easy-going charm about him. He and his wife are still obviously very much in love.

The couple's oldest daughter Joanna, eighteen, is working in Switzerland as an au pair for a year and will be returning to take a Bachelor of Engineering course at Sydney University. Julia, seventeen, who has just left school, is currently thinking over her career options. They are two remarkably attractive, engaging teenagers with everything going for them.

For Mrs Caunt, a well-preserved forty-eight, it could all have been very different. Had the man whom she was going out with more than twenty years ago not been introduced to a girl named

Norma, she could, conceivably, have woken up that morning in London at No. 10. Just a few months after John Major jilted her in 1970, she fell in love with Peter, married before the year was out, and then moved to Wigan where they lived until they made the move to Australia.

'I sometimes think about what I might be doing now if I had married John,' Mrs Caunt says thoughtfully. 'It all seems very glamorous, doesn't it, but then when I give it some thought, think what it would really mean, I appreciate more than ever what I have here. I mean, I had a lucky escape really, didn't I?'

Index

191

INDEX

INDEX

INDEX